the 50
GREATEST
DISHES OF
THE WORLD

IN ASSOCIATION WITH
TIMPSON

Also available

The 50 Greatest Bike Rides of the World

The 50 Greatest Wonders of the World

The 50 Greatest Road Trips

The 50 Greatest Westerns

The 50 Greatest Train Journeys of the World

The 50 Greatest Rugby Union Players of All Time

The 50 Greatest Beers of the World

The 50 Most Influential Britons of the Last 100 Years

The 50 Greatest Walks of the World

Geoff Hurst's Greats: England's 1966 Hero Selects His Finest Ever Footballers

David Gower's Greatest Half-Century

GREATEST
DISHES OF
THE WORLD

JAMES STEEN

Published in the UK in 2017 by
Icon Books Ltd, Omnibus Business Centre,
39–41 North Road, London N7 9DP
email: info@iconbooks.com
www.iconbooks.com

Sold in the UK, Europe and Asia
by Faber & Faber Ltd, Bloomsbury House,
74–77 Great Russell Street,
London WC1B 3DA or their agents

Distributed in the UK, Europe and Asia
by Grantham Book Services, Trent Road,
Grantham NG31 7XQ

Distributed in Australia and New Zealand
by Allen & Unwin Pty Ltd,
PO Box 8500, 83 Alexander Street,
Crows Nest, NSW 2065

Distributed in South Africa by
Jonathan Ball, Office B4, The District,
41 Sir Lowry Road, Woodstock 7925

Distributed in India by Penguin Books India,
7th Floor, Infinity Tower – C, DLF Cyber City,
Gurgaon 122002, Haryana

Distributed in Canada by Publishers Group Canada,
76 Stafford Street, Unit 300, Toronto, Ontario M6J 2S1

Distributed in the USA by Publishers Group West,
1700 Fourth Street, Berkeley, CA 94710

ISBN: 978-178578-173-5

Images – see individual pictures

Typeset and designed by Simmons Pugh

Printed and bound in the UK by Clays Ltd, St Ives plc

ABOUT THE AUTHOR

James Steen is an award-winning journalist and author. A sought-after collaborator with some of the most renowned kitchen legends, he has co-authored the autobiographies of Marco Pierre White (*The Devil in the Kitchen*), Raymond Blanc (*A Taste of My Life*), Keith Floyd (*Stirred But Not Shaken*) and Ken Hom (*My Stir-Fried Life*). He is the author of *The Kitchen Magpie*, and teamed up with Blanc to write *Le Manoir aux Quat'Saisons: The Story of a Modern Classic* and *Kitchen Secrets*, and with White to produce *Marco Made Easy* and *White Heat 25*. During his extensive career in Fleet Street he edited *Punch* magazine. Alongside writing books, he is a contributing editor of *Waitrose Food* magazine. From his home in Wandsworth, South-west London, Steen runs classes for locals in his Loxley Cookery School.

DEDICATION

This book is for Louise.

CONTENTS

For Afters

INTRODUCTION:
BEFORE YOU BEGIN

On a gloriously warm day in autumn 2016, I found myself in Daunt Books, the magnificent, high-ceilinged shop in Marylebone High Street, West London. For once, I was there not to browse the tall shelves and take in the woody scent of new books, but to appear on a stage before an audience and chat with the celebrated chef, Ken Hom, as I had recently collaborated on his autobiography. During the question and answer session, a lady asked Ken: 'What do you think of fusion?'

'Fusion,' he said, with the usual air of Zen about him, 'is fine, as long as it doesn't become confusion.' That single moment remains a vivid memory because, by then, I was deeply immersed in the writing and compilation of the book that you are now holding. Through incessant reading and midnight-oil-burning research, I had become considerably aware – inadvertently – of the true significance of culinary fusion; of how one country's cuisine meets that of another, and results in a new dish.

Fusion may be a comparatively modern term in gastronomy but, as you will see in the pages that follow, for thousands of years it has shaped the food we eat. When the people of one place embrace the people of another, there are marriages, unity and collaboration. Ideas are swapped. New dishes and tastes also come about.

The fusion theme runs through this book, although it was not intentional: I did not set out to write a book about fusion, even if the examples frequently crop up as you read.

Around the time of the chat at Daunt Books, the popular TV chef Jamie Oliver had been castigated by the Spanish because he dared to add chorizo to his paella. 'That's not authentic', screamed his critics. Who was right? The Spanish, or Jamie? As you will see from my entry on paella, the dish may be Spanish, but it would not exist were it not for fusion, admittedly introduced by invaders.

Paella takes its name from the ancient Roman *patella* – think of a paella pan, and that is what the *patella* looked like. The rice was introduced to Spain by the Moors, as was saffron. And the Arabs cannot claim ownership of the rice because that came to them from China and India. Red (bell) peppers are common in paella, but not without the help of the tribes of Aztecs in Central and South America. The peoples of many nations have added a bit of this and a bit of that to paella. So if Jamie Oliver wants to put chorizo in his one, then it is probably allowable.

Paella is not alone; there are plenty more cases. Each and every country, it seems, has a national dish which is influenced by, or has its roots in, another nation.

The ramen of Japan owes so much to the creation of noodles in China, as do you should you be eating noodles this evening. The fish of fish and chips, that classic Great British dish, would not be around were it not for the Jewish immigrants who showed the British how to deep-fry fish in batter. Oh, and it was the Belgians who gave us chips (although the fish and chips were united and first served together in London). The apple pie and the hamburger are surely American-born celebrations, but the first is British and the second is made from beef, not ham, and derives from Hamburg. Would Vietnam have pho, its beefy soup, were it not for the French, lovers of *pot-au-feu*, who occupied their country? Doubtful.

In the course of writing this book, I have made fascinating discoveries. Like most people, I believed that pavlova, that more-ish cake of whipped cream and fruit in a large meringue nest, was invented as a celebratory dessert in New Zealand (or Australia) in the late 1920s when ballerina, Anna Pavlova, toured the Antipodes. This book tells a different story. From the evidence amassed, there is no doubt that a grander version of the cake was being eaten in the Austro-Hungarian Empire of the 1800s, and a pavlova replica was being served in Britain in the late 1800s, when Ms Pavlova was only just entering this world and the grand allegro was a distant leap away.

Beef Wellington has also proved to have had an interesting journey. It may well take its name from the Duke of Wellington but, I have discovered, it seems more likely to have been named by a French chef cooking for the elite of Chicago. He is the one, rather than a British cook, who provided the first recipe. And – improbable though it may sound – was the dish perhaps named Wellington after a Chicago street or avenue? Unfortunately the duke cannot, as has been suggested, have considered this to be his favourite dish, because it had yet to be eaten in Britain by the time he marched heavenwards.

Many of the dishes have been puzzles, but I have tried to establish where each piece fits, and when. Gazpacho, for instance, is a cold tomato soup from Spain ... but it was being made before tomatoes reached Spain. Bouillabaisse is a soupy fish stew from Provence ... but there are recipes which contain no fish. The origins of spaghetti alla carbonara remain a mystery, so who is to say what is and is not an authentic carbonara?

Sometimes the pieces of the puzzle have been lost over time, but I have done my utmost to dig tirelessly, delve deep and explore so that I could present an accurate portrait, a fair biography, of each dish. Food historians do not have all the answers. Where there are questions remaining, I have listed them so that you, too, can have fun and join in the guessing game.

This is not a cookery book, so please do not expect to unearth numerous recipes. Easy recipes, short on words, have been included, as well as historical gems from the dusty but constantly compelling cookery books of centuries past. If, like me, you thoroughly relish such books – partly because they give an entertaining glimpse into the kitchens of the past and what our ancestors ate – then I believe, and sincerely hope, that you will savour this one. And now it is time to put on the oven. Again.

THE 50 GREATEST
DISHES OF THE WORLD

FOR STARTERS

ANTS

Dried first in an oven, the insects can be eaten as a popcorn-style snack, used in meat sauces, or propped up on fresh pineapple chunks to make an unusual dessert in Brazil.

An ant a day, or maybe a handful, is good for you. The ant has long been regarded as medicine, as well as a food. In China, the belief is that what you eat will enable you to inherit the characteristics of the food. If you eat a tiger's penis, for instance, you will be virile. A deer's penis will do, if a tiger is not available. The ant is strong, sexually vigorous and never seems to tire with age. Therefore, eating ants will instil these traits in the consumer.

The *Compendium of Materia Medica* (known to the Chinese as *Ben Cao Gang Mu* or *Pen-ts'ao Kang-mu*) is an impressive masterpiece of some 4,400 pages. It includes remedies and pharmaceutical studies, and was compiled by Li Shizen during the Ming Dynasty in the 16th century. He studied, for instance, the data of 1,094 herbs. You and I might not put ants in the same food genre as parsley, chervil, basil and dill, but Shizen believed they deserved to be regarded as a herb.

Black ants, wrote Shizen, improve our *qi*, or life energy. They make skin beautiful, postpone ageing and restore kidney energy. The millions of people who have followed the advice of the *Compendium* include Emperor Qianlong,

who died in 1799 at the age of 87. He liked to eat black ants, particularly for their anti-ageing properties. With a handful of pine nuts, they were speedily stir-fried in the emperor's wok. The silk-worm chrysalis was another favourite.

Ants were often ground to a paste and eaten with greens. They were eaten by the original natives of Australia, and they are a delicacy in Central and South America, where the earliest tribes harvested the insects for consumption.

Ants have a citrus taste, bitter and acidic; the ant produces an acid to stop predators eating it (the acid is not always successful) and so that is what our palates pick up on. However, ant connoisseurs will be quick to point out that ants are no different to other creatures, in that their taste is affected by the environment in which they have lived, and the diet on which they have survived.

Think of them as having their own *terroir*, similar to wine, tea, coffee and cocoa. Ants from China will taste differently to ants from Thailand, and not all ants in China will taste the same. Some ants are said to be fatty. Large ants are considered to be tastier than small ants, and so it follows that they are more expensive. Of course, you save money by harvesting ants at home, in an ant hill or farming them in a fish tank (minus the water). Once they are collected in a Tupperware box, the box can then be popped into the freezer, dispatching the insects to a chilly demise. Gather the ant bodies and then bake them in the oven on a low heat of about 100°C.

*

Although ants have been eaten for centuries, this ingredient reached haute cuisine status in 2013, when Alex Atala put them on his menu at D.O.M. in São Paulo. The restaurant is frequently ranked in the top ten of the World's Best Restaurants. As one of his desserts, Atala served a dried leaf-cutter ant. Not on its own, but perched on a single cube of fresh pineapple. Simple yet quite beautiful, with an intelligent harmony on the palate while still comprising the essential sweet-sour elements. The dish was witty and fun. The world (the culinary world, that is) took notice.

Atala was not submitting us to a PR stunt. He had discovered the edible joys of ants while travelling in the Amazon. An old lady had offered him a bowl; he tasted and was smitten. 'I found the taste amazing', he recalled. He identified flavours of cardamom, lemongrass and ginger. He was inspired by this new (to him) ingredient. Other ant dishes on his menu have included coconut meringue, topped with an Amazonian ant. São Paulo is the place to go for intriguing ant dishes. At Meats, a burger restaurant in the same city, they serve burgers with vinaigrette of ants.

In Colombia, ants are known affectionately as *hormigas culonas* – literally, big-bottomed ants. They are soaked in a brine before being fried and eaten, usually with a sprinkle of salt. A bit like a tub of popcorn or nuts. They are believed to be an aphrodisiac and are given as a gift at Colombian weddings. Meanwhile, in the mountains of the Santander province, where ants are abundant and cherished, the chefs in the kitchen of the Color de Hormiga (Colour of Ants) rustle up a hearty, protein-rich dish: fillet steak is seared on the grill, covered in ant sauce, and then garnished with dried – you guessed right – ants.

Ants are everywhere. In New York's East Village, for instance, The Black Ant restaurant is a Mexican eatery which serves black ant guacamole, made with mango, avocado, pomegranate, coriander and *chicatana* salt (made from crushed ants). If you don't fancy that, there are other insects on the menu: *Croquetas de Chapulin* are deep-fried parcels of grasshoppers, yucca and manchego, accompanied by grasshopper salsa. With a side order of cactus fries? Mexicans, incidentally, also relish their street food of fried agave grubs, with palm.

*

Turning now to the health benefits. The National Geographic states that a 100 gram serving of red ants provides about 14 grams of protein, which is one gram more than a boiled egg. The same serving of red ants contains 5.7 milligrams of iron, which is 71 per cent of the required daily amount for a man, and about one-third required by a woman. Ants are also a good source of calcium.

The ant is said to be an antiscorbutic: it can prevent scurvy, but only when eaten. The carpenter ant takes its name from the lumberjacks of New England who ate the insects to ward off the illness. Edwin Way Teale, in his Pulitzer Prize-winner *Wandering Through Winter*, mentions that in the early 1900s, Americans could still buy vials of ants as 'a winter's end tonic'.

None of this would have surprised a certain Dr Shreiber, who in Russia in the 1830s, was chief physician at the Brestlitoffski military hospital. What an intriguing character. Dr Shreiber's hospital was surrounded by forest which was home to many ant hills and, *The London Medical Gazette* of June, 1840, reported, 'the thought struck him of drawing some advantage from them for his patients'.

In time, the doctor came up with a treatment for paralysis, although it did not involve eating the insects:

The ants are to be taken directly from their hill and put in a bag; and this bag is to be tied over the limb in such a manner that the ants cannot escape (but obtain access to the skin). Sometime after their application to the limb, the patient begins to feel the running and biting of the ants, by which they gradually excite a kind of electrical twitches, and a feeling of warmth, which gradually extends over the whole body.

This treatment went on for two or three days. The doctor's results were so successful – 46 patients cured over three years – 'that he was encouraged to use the same remedy for rheumatism and gout'. He also used ants to cure a case of elephantiasis; severe swelling of a limb.

The same article in the *Gazette* reveals that in 'Little Russia', the Cossack state, 'they employ a home-made spirit of ants called *muroschkowka*, to prepare a punch which is used in many varieties of colds, with very great advantage'.

*

If you do like to eat ants, you may want to try ant eggs, a topic I covered in an earlier book, *The Kitchen Magpie*. In Thailand, red ant eggs are a versatile and nutritious food whether eaten on their own or as an ingredient in recipes like *Yam Kai Mot Daeng* (a salad), *Kaeng Kai Mot Daeng* (a soup) or *Kai Jiow Kai Mot* (an omelette). Then there is *Kai Mot Daeng Op*, in which lightly salted ant eggs are wrapped in banana leaves before the bundle is roasted.

In Mexico you can sate your appetite with *escamoles*. These are the larvae of ants of the genus Liometopum, harvested from the roots of the country's agave or maguey plants (from which tequila and mescal are made, respectively). In some forms of Mexican cuisine, escamoles are a delicacy, sometimes referred to as 'insect caviar'. They have a cottage cheese-like consistency and taste buttery, yet slightly nutty (those last two terms can also be used to describe caviar). Sometimes ant eggs are thrown in to escamoles, just for that extra crunch.

SMØRREBRØD

A towering open sandwich with a multitude of toppings, many of them pickled or smoked; eaten in Denmark with a chilled shot (or three) of aquavit.

First, a few words about the sandwich in general; two pieces of bread, with a filling in between. The *Oxford English Dictionary* states that the bread should be buttered, although surely butter is an option and not always necessary. A spread such as mayonnaise, mustard, ketchup or HP sauce often eliminates the need for butter. A bacon sarnie does not require butter. Likewise, *Larousse Gastronomique* – the French chef's bible – also ascribes to the buttered bread theory ... but then goes on to list the 'foie gras sandwich', which does not have butter as an ingredient.

The sandwich takes its name from John Montagu, the fourth Earl of Sandwich (1718–1792) and First Lord of the Admiralty. He was also a keen gambler and, so the story goes, during a 24-hour cards session he asked his valet to bring him some roast beef and bread. 'Put the beef between two slices,' he instructed. This, he reasoned, would enable him to eat and continue with the game but would also prevent the cards becoming greasy. (Note: no mention of butter.) His chums marvelled at this spectacularly useful creation.

From that moment on, the cards room echoed with cries of: 'I'll have what Sandwich is having.' Soon it entered the diet of the posh and wealthy, and became dainty finger food.

Of course, Sandwich did not really 'invent' the sandwich, as is commonly suggested. Think of the *paysannes* of France, setting off for a day in the fields. They took with them a bottle of wine, a hunk of crusty bread and a large slice of cheese. Inevitably, the cheese worked its way between the bread. Similarly, Britain's shepherds are likely to have eaten cold meat wrapped in a couple of slices of bread, with an apple or pear for additional sustenance. The *Encyclopaedia of Food and Culture* says of Sandwich: '… During his excursions in the Eastern Mediterranean, he saw grilled pita breads and small canapés and sandwiches served by the Greeks and Turks during their mezes, and copied the concept for its obvious convenience'.

The first known mention of the sandwich comes courtesy of Edward Gibbon, the Member of Parliament, historian and author of *The History of the Decline and Fall of the Roman Empire*. In his journal, snuff-sniffing Gibbon gives the 'sandwich' its debut in print when he records events of 24 November 1762:

I dined at the Cocoa Tree … That respectable body, of which I have the honour of being a member, affords every evening a sight truly English. Twenty or thirty, perhaps, of the first men in the kingdom, in point of fortune and fashion, supping at tables, covered with a little napkin, in the middle of a coffee-room, upon a bit of cold meat, or a sandwich, and drinking a glass of punch.

The sandwich does not seem to feature in a cookery book until 1787, when Charlotte Mason gives it just a nod in *The Lady's Assistant for Regulating and Supplying the Table*. 'Put

some very thin slices of beef between thin slices of bread and butter; cut the ends off neatly, lay them in a dish. Veal and ham cut thin may be served in the same manner.'

*

Digressing briefly, the preceding entries in Mason's 18th century book are for 'Welch' rabbit, Scotch rabbit and English rabbit. Of Scotch rabbit, she instructs: 'Toast a slice of bread of a fine white brown on both sides, butter it; toast a slice of cheese on both sides and put it on the bread.' The 'Welch' rabbit is made in the same way and then '… with a hot salamander, brown it and rub some mustard over it'.

English rabbit, meanwhile, was a boozy affair:

Cut a slice of bread, toast it, and soak it in red wine, put it before the fire; cut some cheese in very thin slices and rub some butter over the bottom of a plate, lay some cheese upon it and pour in two or three spoonfuls of white wine, and a little mustard; cover it with another plate and set it on a chafing-dish of coals two or three minutes, then stir it until it is well mixed; when it is enough lay it upon the bread and brown it with a salamander.

Enjoy!

*

In order to confuse the compilers of the OED and *Larousse*, some sandwiches are still called sandwiches even though they require only one slice of bread, as opposed to two.

This type of sandwich is the 'open sandwich' or 'open-faced sandwich'. The rabbit – be it English, Scottish or Welsh – is not thought of as an open sandwich for some reason. Smørrebrød, however, is. The word stems from *smør og brød*, meaning butter and bread; gastronomy's great understatement of description. Yes, it has butter and bread – rye, pumpernickel, sourdough, white, you name it – as its ingredients, but they are merely the base of the fantastic feast that is piled upon them.

As with a sandwich filling, the smørrebrød can have numerous ingredients, from savoury to sweet. Often it will include smoked fish or meat, and pickled ingredients are frequently used. Cold roasted meats such as pork and beef are popular, as is beef tartare (raw beef, finely chopped).

Onto the buttered bread goes, for instance, smoked salmon, and then prawns, and then sliced hard-boiled egg, and then roe; perhaps a grating or two of horseradish, as well as a slice of lemon and a sprig of dill to garnish. Or maybe you would prefer succulent slices of rare roast beef with fried onions and pickled radishes and a handful of fresh cress. Or sliced potatoes with onion, sliced apple and a couple of sprigs of thyme. Or, for breakfast, a smørrebrød of bilberry jam with whipped cream.

Traditionally this open-sandwich is eaten with a knife and fork, and butter is not essential. But even if that is the case, the dish is still called smørrebrød and not brød. Butter can be replaced by any other fat, and meat dripping is usually the replacement.

The smørrebrød precedes the Earl of Sandwich's sandwich by a few centuries and the bread was probably used as the plate – a pile of ingredients were placed on top, and their juices would be soaked up by the bread beneath. Then the bread, rich in the flavours it had absorbed, was eaten (or not, if you were affluent).

Just as the paysannes of France and the shepherds of Britain left home with their bread and cheese or cold meats, the farm labourers of 17th century Denmark took bread and 'toppings' into the fields so that they had a meal later in the day. This original, but unnamed smørrebrød, was most likely washed down then as it often is today, with Danish beer and a shot of aquavit. In fact, the smørrebrød was being eaten in Denmark before Denmark was even producing butter. The first-known mention appears in the 18th century works of Ludwig Holberg, Baron of Holberg, the Norwegian-born essayist and playwright who spent much of his life in Copenhagen. He does not describe the filling.

At the officers' club in Copenhagen in the 1880s, head waiter Emil Bjorn came up with a list of smørrebrød dishes and handed this menu – or *smørrebrødssedel* – to the officers. They could order and then play cards while eating their open sandwiches. Doubtless, the cards became greasy in a way that would have bothered the Earl of Sandwich. But from this clever move by Bjorn, a new custom was born. These sorts of menus are now commonplace in Danish restaurants.

PHO

A fragrant soup which exemplifies purity of taste. Vietnamese with French influence, the original is made with a stock from beef bones and contains rice noodles.

'Pho is so elemental to Vietnamese Chinese culture that people talk about it in terms of romantic relationships,' writes Andrea Nguyen in *The Pho Cookbook*. 'Rice is the dutiful wife you can rely on, we say. Pho is the flirty mistress you slip away to visit.'

It is pronounced fah – start to say 'fun', which is what the pho is, but stop short of the 'n' sound. Although it is certainly part of the country's culture, it is a comparatively new dish, little more than a century old. It is said that its journey (pho is now popular all around the world) started out in Nam Định, not far from Hanoi, in the North of Vietnam. In the early 1900s, Hanoi was the stopping place for travellers and merchants, and was home to many French men and women. The French had occupied Vietnam since the 1880s (and would remain until 1954), bringing their food customs and cooking techniques. There were also plenty of visitors from the nearby provinces of China. Inevitably, this led to culinary influences, some from the Chinese; others from the French.

The Vietnamese people used cows for work but did not really eat the cattle until they had grown old and were useless. The French, on the other hand, were committed and renowned consumers of beef. Something had to give. So inevitably, the cows were slaughtered. The French took the best cuts, and the remaining bones were retained by the butchers who, in turn, sold them at a cheap rate to the locals. The Vietnamese knew how to make broth, and they applied their skills to the beef bones and carcasses.

They simmered the bones gently for hours and when they had finished they were left with the intensely flavoursome base for the soup that would be called pho. Star anise, chilli, ginger, shallots and coriander were also incorporated. Rice noodles were added, too. Often the dish would have, perhaps, a thin slice of beef, cooked rare in the hot soup. They needed a name for the dish. Pho is believed to be a corruption of *feu*, the French for fire. And while the French make their beloved pot-au-feu – beef with vegetables and stock – in one big pot, so the pho was made in a cauldron: a pot of pho, if you like. It is a one-pot meal.

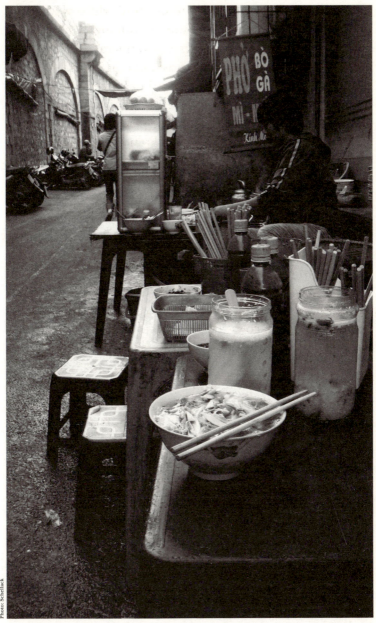

The pho, cheap to make, became street food sold by vendors in Hanoi. Across his shoulders the pho vendor would carry a pole: at one end was the pot of pho; at the other end hung a box containing noodles and spices.

This pho of the North became known as pho bac, and is the first pho. In 1954, when Vietnam was divided, people fled the communist rule of the North and headed south. They took with them their pho recipes and cauldrons. Here in the South, the pho evolved to become pho nam – the pho of the South. Hoisin sauce and fish sauce were added. Beef became merely an option; for the pho nam, chicken could be used instead of cow.

In 1975, at the end of the Vietnam War, refugees fled the country, resettling elsewhere and spreading the word of pho. Once again, it developed: in restaurants around the world, pho is now a dish of extensive variety, and shellfish and pork have joined the long list of possible ingredients.

CAVIAR

The world's most expensive delicacy, originating in the Caspian Sea. The salt-cured roe of the mighty sturgeon is best eaten on spoons made of mother of pearl, with a shot of vodka within easy reach.

This story begins in AD 1240 when Batu Khan (grandson of Ghengis) had finished his annihilation of Moscow, much of central Russia, and Kiev.

With his Mongol warrior's hunger, and a sizeable thirst to quench, Batu went with his wife to Uglich, and to the Resurrection Monastery. There the monks prepared to feed their guests. A feast was brought from the kitchens, one dish after another. There was sturgeon, both roasted at the fire and in a piping-hot soup, and plenty of other dishes, with and without sturgeon as their main ingredient.

Then came the final dish. For this one, apples had been gathered from the trees of the monastery's garden before being stewed. The compote was served with something unknown to the warrior: the salt-cured roe of sturgeon – caviar – was on top of the apple stew. His wife Yildiz did not enjoy the taste, but Batu was overwhelmed by the experience, his first mouthfuls of caviar.

This is the earliest reference to caviar being eaten in Russia, although where and when in the world it was first eaten does not appear in the chronicles of food history. The Greeks, Turkish, Romans and Chinese have all claimed to be the ones who were the first to realise that the eggs taste better than the fish.

The history books can be misleading. They do refer to 'caviar' but caviar back then was not as it is today. Instead, the product was treated as an ingredient, and in one recipe the eggs were used in the same way as the roe of mullet, for instance, to create bottarga (or *poutargue*), of which the Greeks were the pioneers. The roe was taken from the fish immediately after the catch, placed on granite rocks and covered with salt. The elements did the rest: the roe was left to dry in the sun and wind. The eggs were dried, pressed or cooked but never raw salted as they are today.

While the sturgeon was 'royal food', its roe was merely a by-product which was cooked, dried, fried, salted and pressed. It was more of a condiment; an addition to a meal rather than being its very own dish, as it is in the 21st century.

*

In the 1500s caviar had reached Western Europe. The French writer François Rabelais mentioned it in *Pantagruel*, and also described it as the choicest item in what we would now call hors d'oeuvres. And in Tudor Britain, William Shakespeare referred to it in *Hamlet*: 'For the play, I remember, pleased not the million, 'twas caviary to the general ...'

Caviar was not, as Shakespeare and Yildiz Khan would have agreed, to everyone's taste. It was, however, a food that pleased royalty, the elite, and it was rare. Caviar had delicacy status.

In the 1800s it became occasionally talked about in wider, less well-off circles. For instance, in 1837, during the reign of William IV, James Jennings finds room for 'caviare' (it had yet to lose the 'e' of the French spelling) in *Two Thousand Five Hundred Practical Recipes in Family Cookery*.

As you may have gathered from the title, this is an excellent but monumental tome competing to be the heftiest cookbook ever published. Jennings almost runs out of Roman numerals in his Introduction. The subtitle reads: 'In which the whole art of preparing food is simplified and explained, in accordance to the best knowledge of the age, and most conducive to the health and happiness of our species, with an introduction on the duties of cooks and other servants ...'

Of caviar he writes: 'The roe of the sturgeon is usually taken out, put upon a table, beaten flat and sprinkled with salt; it is then dried in the air and afterwards in the ovens; it should be of a reddish brown colour and very dry; this is called caviare and eaten with salt and vinegar.'

Caviar should not be eaten with salt and vinegar. But Jennings was not the only one to promote this as a food which required additions, rather than one that is at its best when eaten on its own. Since the early 1900s, the tradition has been to eat it from a spoon of mother of pearl, or, nowadays, even a plastic spoon. (A silver or stainless steel spoon might taint the roe with a metallic taste.)

*

In British cookery books of this time, sturgeon recipes were more common than references to caviar.

With her characteristic high-spirits, Elizabeth Raffald gave this sturgeon recipe to her readers in *The Experienced English Housekeeper,* published in 1769. 'Take what size of a sturgeon you think proper, and wash it clean. Lay it all night in salt and water. The next morning take it out, rub it well with Allegar and let it lie in it for two hours …' Allegar was a type of sour ale, often used in pickling and the making of catchup (now ketchup).

Raffald also has a recipe for pickling sturgeon in Ale Allegar. Once pickled, the sturgeon is poached in a fish kettle, before the skin is removed and the flesh receives a dusting of flour. Then it is browned in butter and served with a sauce of cream and lemon, and garnished with 'crisp parsley and red pickles'. (On the subject of parsley, quickly, it was used by the Romans, and for centuries it was believed that crowns of parsley were placed on winners' heads at the Isthmian Games. Then it was discovered that the translation was incorrect, and it was wild celery which made the crowns.)

Raffald, and later Jennings, were seemingly unaware that sturgeon was, and is a royal fish. Like whale, it is the property of the English monarch. When Raffald was writing her book, Sir William Blackstone was feverishly producing four volumes entitled *The Commentaries on the Laws of England*, which listed the common laws of the land. The law concerning royal fish had been in place since the 14th century. What's more, in the case of the whale, the king owns the head, and the queen owns the tail. You can catch a sturgeon – and they are to be found in British waters – but the minute you lift it from the water it becomes the property of the monarch. So if you fear the legal repercussions, do not pickle sturgeon at home. This law also reflects the value of sturgeon but notice that caviar is not mentioned because, as with other fish roe, it was often cooked with the fish and had yet to be considered a delicacy.

Indeed, caviar only started to become well known in Russia after 1820 (that was also when the traditional 'original tin' (two kilograms) was created, and the word 'malossol' came into use. This differentiated between the caviar of the day which was pressed and salted heavily, and the one that is less salted, i.e., the malossol.

*

Home for Melkoum and Mouchegh Petrossian was on the Russian side of the Caspian Sea. They had been born in the late 19th century, but on the Iranian side of the sea. At that time the Caspian Sea was divided into five zones, including Iranian waters, and each zone was exploited by one of five Russian families who had been awarded fishing rights by the Tsar.

The Petrossian brothers studied at Moscow University, one to become a lawyer; the other an architect. Their next stop was France, emigrating after the Armenian holocaust in 1915. This was a prosperous era; *les années folles* to the Parisians.

What followed is one of the great fables of entrepreneurialism in 20th century gastronomy. Glancing around, the brothers could see that, although they had left Russia, they were still surrounded by many things Russian. The Parisians had fallen in love, as is the way in that city, with the intriguing cultures of the Petrossians' homeland. Exiled Russian princes were the toast of the town. Russian writers, poets and artists were on the A-list of every giddy, champagned soirée. The arts, the ballet, the choreography of Diaghilev, and the music of Igor Stravinsky; all of it was adored or cheerfully being discovered by the French elite.

The Petrossian brothers noticed, however, that there was no caviar. The delicacy was missing from the lives of their expatriates, and the high society of Paris was mostly unaware of the dark, glistening roe.

The brothers knew the product from their Russian origins (Armenia was part of the Russian Empire). They had no contacts within the new Soviet government to help them arrange an import deal, but they contacted the Russian Ministry of Foreign Trade and were soon told to take cash to the Paris embassy. Hopeful that the Ministry would keep its word, Melkoum and Mouchegh raised the cash and delivered it in two suitcases. Some weeks later the caviar began to arrive.

In 1920, the brothers opened a kiosk to sell their wares. They had realised the value of introducing caviar, and they worked tirelessly to promote and build the brand, using their name on the tins as the trademark, adorned with the now famous red-sailed ship as a logo.

They also turned to César Ritz, the impresario of the European hotel trade, and creator of the Ritz in London. Initially, he was reluctant, believing that it would not sell, and he told them so. (How could he have foreseen then that today, apart from Russia, France is the biggest consumer of caviar?)

Eventually, when caviar went onto the menu at Ritz's prestigious establishment at the Place Vendôme the delicacy caught on quickly. At the 1929 World Exposition, which was held in Paris, the Petrossians had an audience of journalists from around the world. The subsequent positive write-ups helped to establish the reputation of caviar as a luxury item. The company also began to offer other speciality products, such as smoked salmon and foie gras. With business booming, the Petrossians negotiated, through the Soviet Ministry of Fisheries, the exclusive right to import caviar into France, as well as Switzerland, the United States and Canada.

Decades later, the brothers are no longer with us. Yet the Petrossian family continues to oversee the caviar empire (there are a dozen boutiques across the globe). And in 1998, Armen Petrossian became the first French producer to sell farmed caviar (there are about a hundred sturgeon farms in the world). His mother Maïloff was the daughter of one of the five families who had been given fishing rights by the Tsar, and in a sweetly romantic twist she had married Mouchegh Petrossian in 1934.

In about 1935 the Russians established a method of producing sturgeons from wild fertilized roe, and they were the first to release large amounts of the fingerlings into the sea. Most of the world's sturgeon farms were created after 1975, to re-stock the natural habitat. The cost of producing caviar from farmed sturgeon seemed economically impossible, but in 1997 the protection of sturgeon by the Convention of International Trade in Endangered Species created restrictions on the catch. The price of caviar started to jump and saw the beginnings of caviar production from farmed sturgeon.

A year later the world-wide production of farmed caviar was only 500 kilograms. Today it is around 300 tons.

*

There is also a Petrossian warehouse in London, A Touch of Caviar Ltd. Over a tasting of the delicacy, Isabelle Augier, the UK Director, told me that while today's caviar is farmed, the process remains much the same as it has always been.

Of course there are modern improvements. Nowadays, the sturgeon can be scanned by ultrasound to establish the maturity of the roe. When it is time to take the eggs, the fish needs to be despatched in order to acquire the roe. A caesarean can be performed, but afterwards the roe will never be of the same quality.

'The sturgeon's eggs represent more than 10 per cent of the weight of the fish,' says Isabelle. So beluga – the largest species of sturgeon, it can weigh about 100 kilograms and produces the most expensive roe – can produce ten kilograms of caviar. The roe goes from the farm to the shop, and there the process begins. (Italy and China, incidentally, compete to be the largest producers of farmed sturgeon roe.)

'First,' says Isabelle, 'the eggs are put in a sieve and very carefully washed in water. Next, salt is added by hand. Of the total weight, between 2.8 and 3 per cent is salt. The salt brings flavour and is a preservative. Then the salted eggs are packed in what is known as an "original tin". Next, the eggs are gently pressed to release the air. At this point, no more air will be able to get to the caviar. The oil of the eggs, however, can escape through the bottom of the tin, which is what we want to happen. Little by little the residue is expelled. Every so often the caviar is pressed again, and the tin is turned.'

Once in the tin, the maturing starts. 'If you have roe and salt and eat it straight way it will not have the beautiful taste of caviar,' she says.

The eggs from different sturgeon are never mixed. 'Every fish will give a different taste or different sized egg.' The tins are stored at a temperature of -2°C to 0°C.

*

Every Petrossian caviar house has a 'caviarlogue' (a trademarked name). He or she is a sort of caviar master, blessed with an exceptional palate and acute senses, a bit like the tasters of vineyards, distilleries, breweries and chocolatiers. His or her job is to monitor the quality of the caviar, and know when it is just right to sell.

'He knocks the tins to check there is no air inside,' says Isabelle. 'He can understand the maturity of the caviar. He will open the tins to check. He will smell it, look at the colour, the shine. He will smell it and, of course, he will taste it. He is the one who will decide if the caviar is ready to be sold, if it has reached the perfect level of maturity or should it be left, let's say, for another three months.'

Some caviar waits for eighteen months before going on sale, when it is at its best and ready to be eaten. It is the caviarlogue's responsibility to decide the classifications and grades into which each original tin of caviar falls: should it be sold as Royal, Imperial or Special Reserve?

Royal has medium to small sized eggs, firm to melting, with sea flavour notes, and a long and fishy taste in the mouth. Imperial has large to medium sized roe, which are firm, light to dark colour, and subtle aromatic flavours. The Special Reserve is exceedingly rare caviar, selected for its large size roes, and it is aromatic and perfectly balanced. So, for instance, should you have your credit card handy, you might like to buy Ossetra Special Reserve, or maybe Beluga Imperial.

'The country it comes from is not important,' says Isabelle. 'What is important is the species of sturgeon.' The wild species are beluga, ossetra (or oscietra) and sevruga. Farmed sturgeon varieties include baerii and transmontanus. Caviar is subjective – a matter of personal taste. Beluga comes at the highest price because the sturgeon takes about eighteen years to produce eggs, and the eggs are large. Yet the less expensive ossetra, richly buttery, is reckoned to be the connoisseur's caviar.

So as not to break the eggs, caviar should be spooned carefully onto lightly toasted bread or blinis, or directly into the mouth, preferably using that mother of pearl spoon. Place a dollop on the tongue and press against the palate to experience a powerful burst of briny flavours. Some caviar is noticeably acidic, pleasantly so. *La longueur en bouche,* or the 'length' on the palate, signifies good quality caviar: after tasting, the flavours continue to develop in the mouth, in a similar way to a fantastic wine or chocolate.

Keep a clean palate in between mouthfuls; drinking coffee or tea, or smoking while tasting is not recommended. Vodka, brut champagne or a very dry white wine are all acceptable alcoholic companions. Do not eat caviar with eggs or pickles. Add lemon juice if you like, but only at your palate's peril.

Is it time for the bill? The Alba white truffle, to put things in perspective, is an Italian delicacy which sells for about £2,000 per kilo. But that is small change when compared with the price of caviar. In 2016 Harrods charged the following prices for a small tin containing one serving – 30 grams (1.06 ounces) – of caviar: Beluga Imperial, £370; Ossetra Imperial, £110; Baïka Royal, £80; Daurenki Royal, £70.

RAMEN

A nutritious, umami-rich Japanese soup (with ancient roots in China) comprising noodles in a broth that is usually made with pork or chicken stock.

Several thousand years ago in the Qinghai province of northern China there was a settlement called Lajia.

It was a time when water was given God-like reverence. Today we take the availability of water for granted, but then it was the greatest commodity available. Water sustains life, of course, and communities established themselves around rivers, springs, lakes and beside the sea. A source of water was a bit like a church: people gathered close to it. Lajia was one such community, nestling near the banks of the Yellow River. The river kept the inhabitants of Lajia alive but eventually, in about 2,000 BC it would bring catastrophe to the settlement.

From modern scientific studies it seems that one day there was an earthquake and this was shortly followed by the flooding of the river. The town's inhabitants tried to escape a watery fate, but they were trapped and death was instant. The town was buried, much like the disaster of Pompeii in AD 79, when the ancient Roman town was immersed by the eruption of Mount Vesuvius. Indeed, Lajia has become known as 'The Pompeii of the East'.

Lajia and its people were unknown, and would have remained so, were it not for an excavation that started at the turn of this century – some four thousand years after the town was buried. Slowly and carefully, archaeologists and scientists started to unearth the settlement and piece together what it looked like, how it existed and thrived and, of course, how it was destroyed. Archaeologists came across skeletons that were in unusual postures, showing that the inhabitants had died as they tried to flee the flood. From the excavation site, there were touching, haunting photographs of the skeletal remains, one of a mother embracing her child.

Yet Lajia also contained one great secret, which, along with the rest of the town, had been preserved by burial for four thousand years. There among the ruins was an upturned earthenware bowl, which when lifted, revealed a mass of yellow strands, each about 50 centimetres long. The strands were identified as noodles, and they were the oldest ones ever to be discovered. They were evidence that noodles were 'invented' by the Chinese.

Radiocarbon dating of the food confirmed that it was about 4,000 years old. The noodles had been made with grains from millet grass, unlike modern-day noodles, which are made with wheat flour. Scientists examined the shape and patterning of starch grains and seed-husk phytoliths in the bowl, and compared them with modern crops. Their analysis pointed to the use of foxtail millet and broomcorn millet.

'Prior to the discovery of noodles at Lajia,' said Professor Houyuan Lu of the Institute of Geology and Geophysics at Beijing's Chinese Academy of Sciences, 'the earliest written record of noodles is traced to a book written during the East Han Dynasty sometime between AD 25 and 220, although it remained a subject of debate whether the Chinese, the Italians, or the Arabs invented it first.'

The discovery goes a long way to settling the old argument: who created noodles? The ancient food at Lajia resembled the la mian noodles of today. These are made from a dough of flour and water (sometimes a little salt is added). Then, always by hand, the dough is pounded, pushed, pulled, folded, twisted and stretched – and dusted with flour and thumped a few times. Once the dough is perfectly thin, the noodles are pulled from it. 'La mian' means pull noodle. The 4,000-year-old noodles would have been made with millet grain (rather than wheat) and water from the Yellow River (or one of its tributaries).

Slow though it may be, we are heading towards Japanese ramen, I promise.

Photo: yeowatzup

*

In the 8th century BC the Chinese discovered a new form of preservation. They crushed the bones and entrails of shellfish, or fish or game, placed them in earthenware pots and poured in rice wine. Perhaps a little salt was added. There the mixture stayed for a few months, fermentation taking place.

Several hundred years later they discovered that the same fermentation process could be used with soy beans. This they called *jiang*. They also produced a sauce from the process. *Jiangyou* is, literally, the sauce pressed from jiang: known in the West as soy, or soya, sauce, the world's first-ever condiment.

Jiang made its way to Japan in the 6th or 7th century AD. Japan already had *hisio*, a pickled sauce. But now they had jiang, they were on their way to making their very own miso, created from a two-stage fermentation process.

First, steamed grains – brown rice, soy beans or barley – are introduced to a mould, *aspergillus oryzae*, which has been cultivated, usually from rice plants. After a couple of days, the result is what is known as koji and it has the enzymes necessary for the next stage. The koji is mixed with brine – salt and water – and soy beans which have been cooked. This mixture is put into a pot or vat, the lid goes on, and it is left for six to eighteen months.

When the lid comes off, the miso is done: a dark paste which has a meaty taste. This can be added to soups, broths, sauces. It could be added to ramen, when ramen was invented. As with its cousin soy sauce, miso contains umami – the taste, or rather the sensation that instantly lifts our spirits and makes us say: 'Wow!'

La mian also made its way to Japan, but not until the early 1900s, and during the reign of Emperor Meiji. This was an exciting period of innovation in Japan, as feudal society faded away and the country aimed to leave behind its Asian neighbours and catch up with the Western world. An industrial revolution took place, and by the end of World War I the nation was a mighty economic force.

Its food, too, was developing rapidly. There were Chinese restaurants in Japan, and street vendors selling Chinese food. Soon the noodles – inspired by la mian and known as ramen – were introduced to broth or soup. This dish was called *shina soba* (Chinese noodles) but miso had yet to feature in it.

A few hundred tonnes of miso were also being sold annually in America, but that ended abruptly following the outbreak of the Second World War. President Roosevelt signed Executive Order 9066, which permitted the internment of 120,000 west-coast Japanese-Americans. All of the miso shops on the west coast of the United States were forcibly shut down. Their owners and staff, along with other Japanese-Americans, were sent to detention camps.

After the war, the Japanese who had lived in China returned to their homeland, where many of them opened shops selling ramen, and by the 1950s shina soba was a phrase of the past.

The ramen revolution was led by Kazuo Yamagishi, who in 1954 opened his little restaurant, Higashi-Ikebukuro Taishôken. He devised the *tsukemen* (or mori soba) dish: cold noodles served in one bowl, hot broth or soup in the other. You lift some noodles with your chopsticks, swish the noodles around in the soup, and eat. Yamagishi was an interesting eccentric, his head frequently wrapped in a white towel. He died in 2015, at the age of 80, by which time more than 100 of his protégés had gone on to open their own restaurants.

The quality of ramen depends heavily on the pork or chicken stock – it should be exceptional. Ramen is best made in a wok and can be quickly prepared as follows:

First, finely sliced pork or chicken is stir-fried in an extremely hot wok. Finely sliced vegetables – pak choi, lettuce, onion, garlic, lemongrass, you name it – are tossed in, stirred and fried rapidly on the high heat.

The stock, hot, is poured in.

Next, add the noodles. Ramen noodles (which are wheat based, with no egg) are fantastic. Udon or soba noodles will also do the trick. Ladle the soup, with the noodles, into bowls.

Add miso, according to your taste. Garnish with a slice of pork or chicken, and perhaps a slice of hard-boiled egg.

Or follow Yamagashi's route, serving the chilled noodles and soup in separate bowls. Heaven, especially with a bottle of saké.

SUSHI

Japanese 'fingers' of compacted, vinegared rice with finely-sliced fresh, raw shellfish and fish.

About 1,500 years ago, the fishermen of South-east Asia came up with an intelligent and successful way of preserving their catch from the sea, lakes and rivers. They stored the fish in rice, packed tightly in a wooden box and weighted down with a stone. Over the period of a few weeks, the rice fermented and the fish was pickled. The rice would be tossed away, but the pickled fish was there to see the people

Photo: Chatama

through possible famine. Sushi was the name given to the rice, or rather its sour taste.

In the 7th century AD, the technique had spread to Japan, and Lake Biwa, where carp was placed between layers of salted rice. After several months, the rice was removed and the fish was left to cure. This technique was known as narezushi. It was not until the mid-1600s that Dr Matsumoto Yoshici, a court physician, made an interesting discovery: he added rice vinegar in the preparation, which shortened the fermentation process and, quite simply, made the rice taste nice.

But it was a dramatic development involving a street vendor in the 1820s which led to a sushi revolution. Yohei Hanaya sold food to the crowds that came to watch sumo wrestling in Ryogoku, a district of Tokyo. Clearly an enterprising soul, Hanaya devised an exciting type of finger food: finely-sliced raw fish placed on top of compact, vinegared rice, tied together with a strip of seaweed (*kori*). Sometimes horseradish-like wasabi was added. This finger food is nigiri-zushi, known more commonly as sushi.

The crowds were pleased. Very soon others were selling sushi to passers-by. After Tokyo was hit by the earthquake of 1923, many of the vendors left the city and moved to different parts of the country, introducing sushi as they went. Sushi's popularity was boosted on a global scale in the 1970s, when Hollywood stars and Wall Street bankers viewed it as fashionable.

There are different types of sushi, which include maki-sushi: finely sliced fish and vegetables are rolled up in seaweed to form a cylinder, which is then sliced downwards, forming little rolls. Sashimi is slices of raw fish, served without rice (hence no mention of sushi in its name). *Sashi* means to pierce; *mi* is the word for flesh. Dipping sauces often accompany sashimi; these include ponzu, the ingredients of which include rice vinegar and seaweed, as well as the juice of one or more citrus fruits, be it lemon, *yuzu*, or the bitter orange *daidai*. Daidai aids digestion and at Japanese New Year is presented with mochi cakes as a decoration (it is too bitter for most people to eat).

DIM SUM

Prawn dumplings, taro cake and spongy, deep-fried chicken feet. Dim sum in a dim sum parlour is a memorable taste of China.

The Chinese have a saying: 'To be born in Suzhou, to eat in Guangzhou, to be attired in Hanzhou and to die in Luzhou.' Suzhou is a place of great beauty, Hanzhou is home to the finest fabrics and Luzhou has the best wood (for a coffin). Guangzhou, meanwhile, is considered to be home to the best food in China. It is the ancient and capital city of the Guandong province in China's south, an area abundant in great produce and chefs who know how to cook the great Cantonese dishes.

A few thousand years ago, the story goes, five immortals, riding rams that had rice grains in their mouths, flew to Guangzhou on clouds. The immortals blessed the people and promised them glorious harvests for eternity. Thus, it became known as the City of Rams or the City of Rice Grains. It is also said that its culinary reputation was ensured during the overthrow of the Ming Dynasty (AD 1644) when chefs from the imperial household fled south, bringing with them their recipes and kitchen talents.

Guangzhou became an important stop on the Silk Road

of the sea, the network of trade routes which linked China with South-east Asia and later, Europe. In the late 1800s, following the Opium Wars, Guangzhou was the only port open to outside trade. It became rich and its food became known and loved by foreign travellers. Soon the chefs would travel themselves, taking their cuisine across the globe.

The city of the 1800s was not short of restaurants. Many of these were vast and two or three storeys high. The elite dined on the top floor while hoi polloi sat downstairs, eating noodles, roasted meats and soups. All of the customers went into the building via the kitchen. That way, they could check out the cleanliness of the chefs and, of course, see what was on offer, food-wise. Wander through any Chinatown and you will notice the custom continues in the West, with roasting ducks and pigs on view from the street. Apart from these large, often noisy and boisterous restaurants, there was another style of eating out – a visit to the tea salon.

The tea salon was a gentle way to spend an hour or two, and customers would turn up with birds in cages: they competed to see whose bird could sing the sweetest and longest song. To the challenging soundtrack of high-pitched trills, twitters and squawks, waiting staff served pots of tea and little snacks: savoury dishes of minced meat or shellfish in thin-dough dumplings, as well as small, sweet pastries. This was what the modern-day Westerner might call finger food, though always to be eaten with chopsticks and never fingers (at the Chinese table it is rude to handle the food with fingers). These dishes were so delectable, dainty and loveable that, you felt, they almost touched your heart as you ate. Inevitably, they became known as dim sam, or dim sum, the Cantonese for *dot heart*.

Tea salons did not use to be places for women, but nowadays families often spend Sunday mornings there together, enjoying dim sum and tea. Waiters dash about the room, pushing food on table trolleys. Tea is the drink, and when the tea runs out, the lid of the pot is turned upside down – this tells the waiter a top up is required. There are countless types of dim sum. Steamed dumplings might be filled with shrimp or pork, or there is *wu gok*, which is dumpling made with taro. Taro crops up in a dim sum cake, while turnip is grated and mixed with dried shrimp to become a fried cake. Pig sells well. There are steamed pork buns, baked pork buns, pork spare ribs and roast pork and honey wrapped in pastry.

Fung zao are chicken feet, deep fried so that they become spongy and they are served in a sweet-savoury sauce. The toenails should be removed before cooking. Sweet dishes range from *daan taat* (an egg custard tart) and *do fu fa* (tofu pudding) served with a ginger syrup. Fried sesame balls look like round doughnuts, and are filled with red bean paste and covered in sesame seeds.

CHICKEN SOUP

A cure for many illnesses; simmered and ladled by mothers and grandmothers the world over.

Chicken soup was the subject of a scientific study in 1993.

Dr Stephen Rennard, a physician and researcher at the University of Nebraska Medical Center, set out to establish why this particular soup is so good for us. Or, as the study put it: 'A traditional chicken soup was tested for its ability to inhibit neutrophil migration using the standard Boyden blindwell chemotaxis chamber assay with zymosan-activated serum and fMet-Leu-Phe as chemoattractants.'

Moving on …

The study pointed out that chicken soup is 'so widely recommended … in the Jewish tradition, that it is referred to by a variety of synonyms as Jewish penicillin, bohbymycetin, and bobamycin.'

Dr Rennard's wife Barbara, also one of the researchers, played the role of cook. She made three batches of chicken soup. These were prepared according to a family recipe and, for the purposes of the study, the recipe was known as 'Grandma's Soup'. It was typical, traditional chicken-soup stuff. There were no noodles, but there were matzah balls.

Here is the recipe for Grandma's Soup:

A two kilogram chicken is cleaned, put in a large pot and covered with water. The water is brought to the boil. In goes 'a package of' (let's say six) chicken wings; three large onions; one large sweet potato; three parsnips; two turnips; twelve large carrots.

They 'boil' (probably more of a simmer) for one and a half hours.

As scum gathers on the water's surface, it is skimmed and discarded.

Six celery stalks and a bunch of parsley are added.

The whole lot simmers for a further 45 minutes.

The chicken is removed. Its meat is not used for the soup (it can be used in other dishes).

YOU CAN SEE

YOU'RE GOING TO LIKE IT..

BROTH IS RICH WITH *CHICKEN*...

THE RICE IS STEEPED IN *CHICKEN*...

ALL THROUGH IT...THE *CHICKEN*

ou sit down to a steaming plate of soup, what you want above all is— And that, in Campbell's Chicken what you get above all. Plenty of

chicken goes into its making—fine plump chickens simmered ever so slowly to make a broth that fairly gleams with chicken richness. Fine white rice, cooked to fluffy

lightness, is then added to the broth finally, pieces of chicken are meas generously, chicken so deliciously te just about melts in your mouth.

at's Why—

AS SURE AS YOU LIKE CHICKEN, YOU'LL LIKE *Campbell's* CHICKEN S

Salt and pepper are added to your taste.

The soup is strained and the vegetables are finely chopped or passed through a strainer. Salt and pepper are added to taste.

Note: The report states that, 'No strict quality control was performed, although each preparation was evaluated by taste and was felt to be satisfactory (if variably so).'

*

The study, which was presented at a conference in San Francisco, set out to show scientifically that chicken soup is good for the immune system and prevents colds.

None of the findings would have surprised, for instance, the Egyptian Jewish physician and philosopher, Moshe ben Maimon who, in the 12th century, recommended chicken soup for respiratory tract symptoms (and ben Maimon's advice was based on earlier Greek writings).

But Rennard's point was that there was little in the literature to explain how chicken soup is so good for us.

'Everyone's heard this from their mother and grandmother in many cultures,' he said, but he wanted to demonstrate the soup's anti-inflammatory properties.

The study concentrated on neutrophils. These are the most common white cells in our blood and they defend the body against infection. The study's focus was to find out if the movement of these neutrophils would be blocked or reduced by chicken soup. A reduction of movement is beneficial to the body.

The researchers collected neutrophils – white blood cells – from blood donated by healthy volunteers. During tests they found the movement of neutrophils was reduced, suggesting that chicken soup does have an anti-inflammatory 'activity'. This may ease symptoms and shorten upper respiratory tract infections. If you've caught a cold, drink the soup and you'll feel better.

'A variety of soup preparations were evaluated and found to be variably, but generally, able to inhibit neutrophils,' Dr Rennard said.

The researchers were unable to identify the exact ingredient or ingredients in the soup that made it effective against fighting colds. But they believed it may be a combination of ingredients in the soup that worked together to have beneficial effects.

As part of the study, thirteen shop-bought chicken soups were also tested against Grandma's Chicken Soup. 'Many of the soups inhibited neutrophil chemotaxis. Five inhibited more potently (at an identical dilution) than did Grandma's traditional soup. Two soups were without activity, and one slightly augmented chemotaxis.' The report added, 'Omaha tap water had no activity.'

FISH AND SHELLFISH

FISH AND CHIPS

'Salt and vinegar?' Three words which every night echo around Britain's 27,000 chippies.

The chip was most probably introduced to Britain in the

Photo: Gill Rickson

mid-1800s by the Belgians. But it had to wait a while to be united with the fish.

That happened in about 1860 with the opening of the nation's first fish and chip shop. The man behind the business was Joseph Malin, a Jewish immigrant and cook who lived in the impoverished East End of London.

His shop was located at 450, Old Fort Street, in Poplar. It was a working class area, inhabited by labourers, servants and railway workers. But then fish and chips has always been a working class treat, and it is only recently that it has become a fixture on the menus of Michelin-starred restaurants.

Trade was strong (Malin's customers, perhaps, included couples who came to walk on Sundays in the park opposite his shop) and word spread. Britain now has 27,000 fish and chip shops (also known as chippies, fish shops or chip shops). And while Malin's marriage of deep-fried fish with chips is loved around the world, his name has not travelled further than a gravestone in the land of cockneys.

What of the fish? In the 17th century fried fish was introduced by Jewish immigrants who came to Britain from Portugal and Spain. Here is Paul Levy, writing in the *Daily Telegraph*:

> Claudia Roden's 1996 *The Book of Jewish Food*, the ultimate authority, says battered fried fish 'was a legacy of the Portuguese Marranos (crypto-Jews) who came to England in the 16th century, many of them via Holland'. Nominal Christians, they were secretly practising Jews, who fried their fish on Friday (the Christian world's fish day) and ate it cold on their Sabbath later that night or the next day, when they were forbidden to cook or even light a fire.

Originally, the fish was dipped first in egg and flour before frying. Batter, however, was a far better preservative and became a popular coating. Batter – a mix of egg, flour and milk – has been around since medieval times, featuring in savoury and sweet, often fruity dishes. Without it, there would be no American pop-over, French cherry clafoutis, or English puddings, such as Kentish cherry batter pudding or Tewkesbury saucers: a sort of fruit sandwich made with two small pancakes.

PAELLA

A huge pan of saffron rice, shell-on prawns and opened mussels, maybe some chicken thighs or pieces of rabbit, as well as red (bell) pepper and wedges of lemon. Entirely Valencian, of course.

You are a cook in ancient Rome and you awake one morning with a desire to cook, not for the family, friends or neighbours, but for the gods. You're not quite sure what to make, but you know for sure which utensil to cook it in. You raid the kitchen cupboards, with dust dirtying your toga, and pull out the *patella*. That's the one!

The large *patella* was bronze, large, concave-based and had two handles. It was fit for the gods and great feasts. Otherwise, it could be the vessel for a simple but impressive supper with the neighbours al fresco.

When the Romans invaded the Iberian shores and settled in Valencia, on the south-east coast of Spain, they unpacked *patellae* galore. The *patella* dropped a 't' to become *paella* and it even increased in diameter, enabling the pan to sit

Photo: Carlos Delgado

comfortably on a long-burning fire of small branches and twigs. (Up until the 16th century the French called their pan a *paele* before it became *poêle*). The *paella* is made from iron, never known as a *paellera*, and originally the Valencians used it to fry fish and meat with vegetables. (The 'll' of paella is pronounced as either the 'lli' in million, or as a 'y' – pie-ay-ah. It is never pie-ella.)

Next, the Moors pitched up in Valencia in the 8th century. From North Africa and the Near East they brought trees of oranges and almonds. They planted expansive plantations of sugarcane. They brought a cultured lifestyle enriched by poetry, art and architecture. They introduced an irrigation system that would help to increase farmland, crops and improve health. And by the time King Jaime of Aragon liberated Valencia in 1238, the Moors had created vast and fertile fields of rice – paella's advent had occurred. Spain had a new food with a new word – *arroz* (rice) originates from *ar-ruzz*, the Arabic word.

Although conceived in Spain, paella was therefore a gastronomic collaboration of the Romans, the Moors and the Valencians. Indeed, there is a strong case for bringing China and India into it too, as that is where the rice travelled from, to the Moors. Paella is a shining example of what, hundreds of years later, would be known as 'fusion food'.

The early paella consisted of rice from the fields, onions, garlic and rosemary from the garden, and fish and seafood – mussels, squid, octopus – fresh off the coast. Perhaps, after a hard day's toil of rice harvesting, it was cooked on a fire beside the fields, snails tossed in as well. Traditionally, it is cooked by men and indeed there are those who say (erroneously) that the dish takes its name from the words *para ella*, for her (as in, here is a meal that was made by a man for his wife).

The essential saffron, another gift from the Moors (and originating from India), makes the paella a smiling sun within a black halo.

*

Digressing for a moment, saffron is ridiculously expensive – in fact, the most expensive spice – and that is because of its laborious harvest. It comes from the stigmas of crocuses which have to be picked by hand. The strands are extracted from the flowers, and then dried. When used in dishes, saffron adds a wonderful aroma and a highly appetising yellow-orange colouring. (Some cooks add turmeric instead of saffron: this will colour the rice, but it's a cheap trick because one mouthful and you know the saffron is missing and you've been duped.)

In the 16th century, the European fascination for spices saw the cultivation of saffron across the continent. It was grown in Britain, and the Essex town of Saffron Walden was simply Walden before its inhabitants started growing saffron in the 16th century. Saffron cakes, bread and buns are still often eaten in England. In Devon, they baked 'revel buns' which contained saffron and were eaten at church feasts known as revels. Should you find yourself in Sweden on 13 December, do not be alarmed if you are approached by young girls dressed in white robes with crowns of lingonberry twigs, carrying trays of cakes and saying *'Lussekatter'*. They are celebrating the feast of Santa Lucia and the delicious, plaited buns are made of saffron, currants, nuts and candied peel. Lussekatter means Lucia's cats, the name given to the buns.

Take bun dough, place it in the oven and see how it swells and contemplate the origin of the word *bun*. It derives from *bugne*, the Old French word for swelling. A *bugne* in the oven.

Elizabeth David, in *French Provincial Cooking*, writes that 'about 500,000 pistils, or about 170,000 flowers, go to make up one kilo of dried saffron, which goes to show why saffron is so expensive and why it has often been falsified'. Before use: soak half a dozen pistils, or threads, of saffron in a little hot water allowing them to infuse and turn the water yellow-orange. This liquid, along with the threads, is added to the dish.

*

Rabbit, chicken and pork were later additions to paella, something of a luxury to the Valencians who lived mostly on a diet from the sea. Tomato and red (bell) pepper would also be incorporated but, of course, only after they started to make their way from the Americas to Spain in the 1600s.

When King Jaime arrived in Valencia, having gone to a great deal of trouble to capture the city, he was surprised to find rice fields all over the place. He feared constant malaria epidemics would eventually result in a city with no inhabitants. So he ordered rice cultivation to be restricted to the Albufera lagoon area.

This brings us to the rice, which is paramount to the success of paella. The wrong rice will render it a failure because the authentic flavour will not be acquired. (A few notable Spanish cookery books suggest long grain rice, but it is not quite right.) The Bomba variety, which is cultivated in this part of Spain, is perfect for paella. Calasparra is the second best. (For risotto, use Carnoroli, which is far less gloopy than Arborio and distinctly superior).

When cooking this dish, as with any rice or pasta dish, imagine that you are 'feeding' the rice: each liquid which is added will be lapped up by the thirsty carbohydrate, adding layers of flavour to the finished dish. Unlike risotto, when the rice is heated in the pan before liquid is added, paella calls for the rice to be added to the bubbling liquid.

Note: Paella is not the only dish which takes its name from the utensil in which it is cooked. The French who went to settle in North America and Canada in the 17th and 18th centuries, travelled with *une chaudière*, a trusty iron cooking pot, perfect for thick soups made with a hearty hotchpotch of ingredients.

In their new homeland, and in between farming and furrier duties, the settlers used ingredients which were new to them but popular with the Native Americans. And so, with the unity of American ingredients and French culinary technique (and cooking equipment), a new form of soup was created in the chaudière. It was chowder. Globally, New England's clam version is the most famous, but seafood can be swapped for vegetables such as sweet corn. Potato helps to thicken the soup.

HÁKARL

Nose pegs on! Here comes the putrid but character-building shark meat of Iceland.

Hákarl is the dish which has defied disgust. By some remarkable feat of endurance, it has survived the centuries since its invention and continues to be produced – and eaten – even though its taste is arrantly revolting, its aroma utterly repugnant. There are legends about hákarl and how it is made.

This dish is, quite simply, the fermented flesh of the Greenland shark. Some describe it as 'putrid'. The meat of this species is poisonous when raw.

To make it – and I hesitate before using the word – *edible*, it is chopped into pieces which are then tightly wrapped in cloth or paper and buried in the ground. There they stay for anywhere between one and three months, undergoing a fermentation process: a reaction of enzymes which, in this case, kills the toxins in the meat and renders it tender and digestible. The meat is then unwrapped and left to dry in the sun for a few weeks. There are Icelanders who consider it unnecessary or even wrong to bury the meat: instead they cut it into strips which are hung in the elements.

Either way, once preserved it can be stored away in a dark cupboard and brought out for special occasions or just nibbles. The 'rind' is not eaten. If you lack olfactory sensory neurons, or are courageous enough to ignore the smell, you will notice that the beige meat has a fatty texture, and the after-taste is fishy.

Shark is not always an unappealing fish to eat, and edible species include Hammerhead, Angel and Dogfish. Shark fin is a delicacy in China, and believed to give strength to the consumer. It is served in a chicken broth; the quality of the broth gives flavour; the fin has little taste but brings a gelatinous texture much appreciated by the Chinese.

There is a debateable and controversial element to the story of hákarl: apart from being buried, is the shark meat also doused in human urine? The ammonia of urine is said to assist the cure and to neutralise the nasty pong of ammonia in the flesh. Urine is also high in salt, which would aid the cure of the shark meat.

During my first and, sadly, only visit to beautiful Iceland, I raised this subject with a member of staff at the tourism board. She said,: 'My grandfather used to make hákarl. He wrapped the shark meat in newspaper and then buried it under rocks. Every now and again, he would dig up the newspaper bundle and urinate on it. Then it was returned to the ground. He loved to eat it.' Others have also told me of this peculiar custom.

By contrast, I have since been told by another Icelander that 'this practice, if it did happen, certainly does not happen any longer'. So step back, Health and Safety. Yet hákarl continues to be the subject of myth and fable.

There is no doubt that it possesses a taste which has yet to be acquired by most visitors to the country, and many of its 332,529 inhabitants (particularly the younger generation).

However, it is served by hip chefs in the capital city of Reykjavik, which food-wise is home to only a few restaurants, and a stationary van by the port which sells Icelandic frankfurters to a never-ending queue.

Hákarl is sliced into little bite-sized cubes, but even though intriguing to the eye, this presentation does little to diminish its wretched effect on the other senses. The prosecution calls two witnesses, both renowned gourmets and men who would consider themselves capable of eating anything.

First, Dan Doherty, executive chef at the Duck & Waffle in the City of London. He winces as he recounts to me his experience of this dish: 'It came to the table as a small cube in a jar. I opened the jar and the smell of ammonia was so strong that it burnt my nose. I put the cube on my tongue and it started to fizz. I ate it in one go, and then necked a whole pint of beer. It was absolutely horrific.'

Second, Heston Blumenthal, owner of the three-Michelin-starred Fat Duck in Bray-on-Thames, Berkshire. He remains shocked by the Icelandic delicacy. 'Two of the most bizarre foods of my life were tasted in Iceland, and within two days

Photo: Austin Matherne

of each other,' he tells me. 'First there was *hákarl*. One mouthful and I thought I was in anaphylactic shock. It was horrific.' (His second most bizarre food was *skata*, 'which is skate and smells like it's rotting. It was as if my throat was suddenly controlling my body and saying, "I'm not eating that!" I spat it out.')

Aside from hákarl, Iceland has excellent lamb (the testicles, when boiled, are a delicacy) and dairy produce, including *skyr*, a very tasty, creamy yoghurt, which is served with berries and enjoyed at breakfast but can also double as a dessert. Skyr has become a popular export, now found in the chilled section of many supermarkets in Britain.

Minke whale is cut up and cooked as huge steaks, or finely sliced and eaten raw as the Icelandic version of *carpaccio*. This can be found at The Grill Market restaurant, a popular eatery in Reyjavik, which also serves small burgers made from puffin.

Reindeer, meanwhile, makes a hearty stew, or is turned into mincemeat patties, which are fried and placed in between a couple of slices of bread. Sheep's head – a popular dish in Britain, but not since Edwardian times – is a treat, and the Icelanders make it into a spread which is smothered onto hot toast. The blood of the sheep is used to produce blood pudding – a bit like Britain's black pudding – which is sometimes eaten with sugar sprinkled over it. Other customary dishes include fish guts and cod's tongues.

The cold weather is firmly addressed by shots of lethal alcoholic drinks. Hákarl is usually washed down with *brennivin* ('burning wine'), a type of schnapps made from potatoes and caraway seeds. Iceland also produces potent spirits which are concocted from the bark of birch trees – *birkir*, which is quite bitter, and *björk*, which, like the Icelandic singer of the same name, is sweet. A shot or two is said to improve skin, hair and sex drive. Any more than that; expect the reverse effects.

BOUILLABAISSE

A big, bright bowl of Provence, made with fish, shellfish, saffron and olive oil; adorned with a dollop of rouille, and served with crunchy, garlicky croutons to soak up the soup.

Do you ever yearn to be in lavender-scented Provence or the aniseed-fragranced South of France? One spoonful of bouillabaisse will zoom you there in a flash. It combines not just a couple of flavours of the Mediterranean, but unites a multitude of them. And successfully so; there are no clashes of taste in this soupy stew.

Each cook, however, makes it similarly but differently, which means that there is, as such, no authentic recipe. In 1960 Elizabeth David observed:

> Every French gastronomic writer and cook for the past hundred years (and some before that) has expounded his theories on the dish so beloved of the Marseillais, and each one gives his own recipe – the only authentic one. And, however many Marseillais, Toulonnais, Antibois, or other natives of Provence you ask for the correct recipe, you will never receive the same instructions twice.

There are three common rules. First, you might need to be in Provence to make it particularly well, as the best

Photo: smallkaa

bouillabaisse requires fish which is fresh-out-of-the-water fresh. Second, the oil (always olive oil), water and wine must be boiled to form an emulsion. Third, the fish and shellfish must not be spared – or so you would think. There are in fact a couple of accepted Provençal recipes for bouillabaisse that do not contain fish. Elizabeth David insists that 'rascasse is essential, and the fish is always served with its head'.

Bouillabaisse stems from *bouillon abaissé*, literally 'broth lowered': the soup 'reduces', lowers in volume, as it simmers and the liquid evaporates. It may well have started life as a fisherman's dish, cooked on the beach in one large, black pot or cauldron. In his *Oxford Companion to Food*, Alan Davidson cites the first known recipe as appearing in 1830 (in *La Cuisine Durand*). Entitled 'Bouillabaisse à la Marseillaise,' its ingredients featured expensive sea bass and spiny lobster.

The choice of Mediterranean fish is yours. With sheer love for this dish, Rick Stein makes a superb version with monkfish tails, fillets of gurnard and John Dory, lobsters (using the thinner legs, with fish bones, for the stock), conger eel and pollack. He enriches the dish with its other traditional ingredients: white wine, tomato purée, *bouquet garni* (a small bundle of thyme, parsley and bay leaf), garlic and, of course, saffron (without which, I believe, this dish could not be called bouillabaisse).

Stein adds a kick or two by incorporating dried chilli powder, cayenne pepper and curry powder. It is cooked for about an hour, and the most tender of the fish is added towards the end as it requires little cooking. Traditionally bouillabaisse is served with rouille (mayonnaise enriched with puréed potato or roasted red (bell) peppers and garlic). 'Bouillabaisse without rouille,' so the saying goes, 'is like Provence without sunshine.' Croutons, which can be rubbed with garlic, are tossed on top of the dish, or served on the side.

The lobster and other shellfish are often served as a first course, in a bowl with the soup poured around it. The fish is dished up as a main course, perhaps with a fantastic salad of coarsely-sliced Marmande tomatoes, fennel and black olives.

*

Raymond Blanc was raised in the Franche-Comté region of France, but will never forget his first visit, aged twelve, to Provence, to see his friend René – and his discovery of bouillabaisse. In *A Taste of My Life* he speaks with wondrous passion of how he watched René's mother, Madame Simon, cook the dish:

In Franche-Comté my mother used butter, and sometimes vegetable oil. Here, in Provence, Madame Simon used olive oil, which went into the large casserole followed by chopped onions, garlic, bay leaf, thyme, celery, and was it fennel? … In Franche-Comté we had tarragon, chives, chervil, parsley, bay leaves and thyme. René's mother cooked with Provençal favourites like rosemary, fennel, basil, marjoram, coriander, star anise and saffron.

Once the vegetables and herbs were sweetened, she added the rock-fish and the saffron. The chopped tomatoes went in too, along with a generous splash of white wine. I remember being intrigued when she added a splash of pastis, the alcoholic aniseed drink, because although I had seen it drunk before I had absolutely no idea it could be used in cooking. Then the ingredients were covered with water and simmered for twenty or thirty minutes, just enough to cook them and create the exchange of flavours. After that she pushed the soup through a mouli.

While the soup was cooking Madame Simon made the aïoli, that delicious garlic mayonnaise made with the best extra virgin olive oil. If you add saffron and puréed potato you will have a rouille. Both reek of garlic, and you wonder why the French are in such rude health.

There you have your fish soup, which can be served with a spoonful of the aïoli and croutons rubbed with garlic. This soup was also a base to cook the fillets of rascasse and lotte. Then it becomes a bouillabaisse, and it was this that Madame Simon made for us. A bottle of rosé, the local Bandol, was uncorked to toast the reunion.

Of the feast, Blanc is almost licking his lips as he concludes: 'In one mouthful I discovered all these new flavours, as well as having my first taste of bouillabaisse.'

*

Sometimes cooks are frightened by the prospect of cooking fish. Moules Marinière is a great dish for beginners and will build confidence because it is so simple to make. All you need (to serve four) is a kilo of fresh mussels, 150 millilitres dry white wine and 100 millilitres double cream. Cider can be used instead of wine. The dish will also benefit from a few sprigs of thyme or any of your favourite fresh herbs. But no other ingredients are necessary, and certainly no salt as that'll be inside the shells of the mussels.

Begin by washing the mussels under cold running water to remove any grit. Pull away any seaweed 'beards' which are protruding through the shell. Discard any mussels which are open but which don't close when you tap the shell. If they don't close it means they are dead. You want live mussels.

Heat a casserole dish or large saucepan (which has a lid). Pour in the wine, bring it to the boil and let it boil for about twenty seconds. Add the mussels. Put on the lid to let the mussels steam over a medium-high heat for four minutes. Lift the lid. If all the mussels have opened, they are done. Pour in the cream, add the herbs, put on the lid and give the pan a good shake. Discard any mussels which have not opened.

Serve immediately with a baguette that can be happily ripped apart at the table.

CEVICHE

A light, refreshing, South American dish in which the finely-sliced flesh of fish or shellfish is marinated, typically for only a matter of minutes, in citric juice.

Ceviche may well be one of the earliest ways of preparing food for consumption, as well as preserving it. The technique requires no heat, and just two ingredients: fish and the juice of citrus fruit.

There you are, a savage foraging and scavenging around in early civilisation, searching for the next piece of food. You catch a fish from the sea, or gather some shellfish. You pull it apart with your fingers, tear strips from the flesh and pluck a lime from the branch of a tree. You squirt the lime juice onto the fish, unaware, of course, that a few thousand years later scientists would identify this as the 'denaturing' process caused by the citric juice. It is not cooking as no heat is applied to the fish, but the acid has a similar effect to heat

CEVICHE

Photo: José Porras

on fish, in that it breaks down the protein. The sousing of the fish also preserves it.

But ceviche is not as old as it might seem, surfacing comparatively recently, in the 1500s.

It originated in South America, possibly Peru. One theory is that, following their 16th century conquest of Peru, Spaniards introduced lemons to the Incas, as well as the Spanish custom of using lemon as a seasoning (which, incidentally, is often a healthy replacement to salt). Soon afterwards ceviche came about (it sounds similar to the Spanish fish stew, cebiche). Others point to an Arabian influence.

The dish is easily made: usually the fillet of the fish is sliced finely, and the citric juice is squeezed over it. A few minutes later, depending a little on the type of fish, it is ready to eat. But from that ceviche base, embellishments and other ingredients and seasonings can be added.

Most South American countries have their own ceviche dishes. Shark and sea bass are favourites for ceviche in Peru, where it is served with corn on the cob and potatoes. In Costa Rica they make ceviche from mahi mahi and marlin, while Chile opts for halibut and Patagonian toothfish. Ecuador ceviche uses the flesh of crab and octopus. Some use the juice of lemon; some use the juice of lime, and some use the juice of orange. Onions, garlic, peppers, tomatoes – all of them can be added, or served as an accompaniment. In Hawaii, soy sauce is a favourite. Olive oil can be added to the juice at the point of marinating. Another Spanish influence? White-fleshed fish are best. A snip of coriander often improves the dish. For many, ceviche (or seviche) may seem to have appeared from nowhere, and then become a modern-day food trend. But it has caught on. The Spanish, of course, eat it; and Britain has a growing number of Peruvian restaurants, many of them called ceviche-something-or-other.

Ceviche is not to be confused with escabeche, in which fish is first fried and then mixed into a vinegar sauce. This practice is used in Spain and Italy and, although it crops up in Britain's 17th century cookbooks, clearly it did not catch on and is not a common cooking technique in the United Kingdom. If mushrooms and/or red (bell) peppers are added to the vinegar the result is a sweet and sour taste, and there are similarities with ketchup, which is believed to have come from China, the Chinese being great admirers of the sweet-sour taste.

LOBSTERS THERMIDOR AND NEWBERG

A pair of classic 19th century dishes, in which pieces of lobster are served in creamy sauces. Luxurious and indulgent.

Lobster Thermidor is the French cousin of America's Lobster Newburg. They are made in a similar style, and both were created by chefs in restaurants – Thermidor in Paris, Newburg in New England – in the 1800s. Each has a bewitching story of drama – what some might call a curse – behind its creation. For both, the lobster is first cooked (either grilled or boiled), and then the flesh is removed and sliced into thick pieces. Each dish is served in a sauce, at which point they differ.

Thermidor sauce begins with a base of Béchamel sauce (also known as white sauce), made by combining flour and butter in a saucepan, to which milk is added slowly, first stirring and then whisking (by hand, with a balloon whisk) and seasoning well with salt and white pepper, to create a glossy, custard-thick sauce. Very finely sliced shallots may be used at the flour–butter stage. Cream is added to enrich the sauce, and bring a silky texture. A little white wine or white wine vinegar may be added to the finished Béchamel, for acidity and to create depth of flavour. Herbs, such as tarragon or parsley are optional. Fish stock (or fish 'fumet') is often included: it is strained through a sieve, and incorporated with the Béchamel.

Thermidor sauce is then finished with Dijon mustard, to your taste. Sometimes cheese is added to the hot Béchamel. While various chefs suggest cheeses such as Parmesan, if you intend to head down the cheese route, then Gruyère works well here. If using cheese, add salt to the sauce when it is finished, as Gruyère will introduce its own saltiness. Auguste Escoffier succinctly concludes: '… In the bottom of the two half shells, replace the slices of lobster neatly on top and coat with the sauce. Glaze lightly in a hot oven or under the salamander [grill].'

America's Lobster Newburg tends not to be served in the shell, but on its own, and sometimes on toasted bread. As with Thermidor, the shellfish is first cooked, the pieces of flesh are removed from their shell and then they are sautéed quickly in a pan with clarified butter on a medium-high heat. No more than half a cup of Madeira (or cognac) is added and reduced over a boil. Then the heat is turned down and a mixture of cream and egg yolks is poured in and stirred over the gentle heat; it should not be allowed to boil. Continue to stir until the sauce has thickened. Add cayenne pepper and a little more butter, stir again. Taste, season if necessary, and serve (sometimes on the toast).

Of course, there have been numerous variations since these dishes were created. A spoonful of caviar, for instance, is added if the cook is feeling extravagant. Tabasco is sometimes added to Newburg. But essentially they are at their best when they are not too fussy, and neither calls for fancy accompaniments. A vibrant green salad is the perfect partner.

From their creation, both dishes were instant hits, particularly illustrative of the rich tastes from the early 1900s to 1920s, and for decades they were highly popular in restaurants in France, America and Britain. They epitomise the Escoffier style, even though he did not have a hand in their inventions. American lobster (Homarus americanus) and European lobster (Homarus gammarus) are the only 'true' lobster species. They have smooth shells and large front claws. Their shells, which can be blue, brown or even green, turn red when cooked. While spiny (or rock lobster) has sweet, firm meat, the American and European species have a richer, more savoury flavour.

Over the past couple of decades, Thermidor and Newberg have slowly vanished from many menus. People have lost an appetite for lobster in restaurants, possibly because it is considered too expensive for both restaurant and diner. But combine the expense with the fact that – let's face it – lobster is brutally destroyed when in the wrong hands. It can be easily overcooked and therefore ruined. Once ruined, there is no sauce, be it an exquisite Thermidor or a superb Newburg, which can bring lobster back to life on the palate.

So ordering lobster from a menu became something of a gamble. You and I, let's say, are visiting a restaurant for the first time. It seems a nice place, but we have no idea of the quality of the food. The restaurant could be great, or it could be dreadful. On the menu, there is Lobster Thermidor or Lobster Newberg, as well as a choice of steaks. We have the menu in our hands and mentally, of course, we weigh up the odds; lobster or steak? We like both. But which one is the chef likely to get right? Or, if you are a pessimist, which one

Photo: Ranjith-chemmad

is the chef most likely to mess up? Either way, we shall most likely opt for steak. The history of lobster, unfortunately, proves it.

That is one of the reasons why steak is on so many menus in Europe and the States, and why there are so many steak restaurants. When did you last see a lobster restaurant? And if you are a restaurateur with Lobster Newburg on the menu, but no one is buying it … Well then, you will remove it from the menu to save yourself from going bust.

It is quite simple to train a chef to cook the perfect steak, and steak does not use up much space in a professional kitchen. Lobster takes up space and it must be kept alive before it is cooked. Think of those times when you have eaten lobster and it is spongy. Chances are, the lobster was cooked when it was stone cold dead. It should be live, or have been recently alive, when it is immersed into the big pot of bubbling, boiling water.

*

Newberg is the eldest of the two dishes. The story begins with Ben Wenberg, who was a merchant seaman, trading in fruit which he bought in Cuba and sold in New York. Or he was a broker in downtown Manhattan. Whatever his profession, he liked to eat at Delmonico's restaurant and became friends with the owner Charles Delmonico, the latest in a line of Delmonicos to run the restaurant since it opened in the 1820s. Anyhow, one day in 1876 Wenberg was having lunch and mentioned to Delmonico that, on his travels, he had eaten lobster which was cooked in an unusual way. Wenberg was kind enough to cook the dish, in order to show the restaurant owner how it was made.

In *Delmonico's: A Century of Splendor*, Lately Thomas writes:

A man who witnessed Ben's initial preparation of the dish recounted the scene thirty years afterwards, and recalled particularly that at the end Wenberg took from his pocket a small flask, and shook into the pan a little of the reddish powder it contained – the inevitable 'secret ingredient'. Delmonico's cooks were satisfied that the stuff was only cayenne pepper, though Ben never told. This same witness of Wenberg's first demonstration maintained that the dish, when 'made to perfection,' should contain only 'lobster, sweet cream, unsalted butter, French cognac, dry Spanish sherry, and cayenne pepper.'

The restaurant employed French chefs, one of whom was given the task of replicating the cooking style and perhaps adding a few touches. That explains the classical French style of this dish, and the incorporation of plenty of butter and the reduction of Madeira. It is all very French. The dish went onto the menu with the fruit trader's name attributed to it. People came just to try this wonderful new dish 'Lobster à la Wenberg'. Some months later, Delmonico and Wenberg fell out. They had a row, the subject of which is still a mystery. The dish was selling extremely well, and perhaps Wenberg asked for a cut of the significant profits from the dish. Who knows? But the fall-out was bitter enough for Delmonico to rewrite all the menus, changing the name of the dish from Lobster à la Wenberg to Lobster à la Newberg. The recipe was in cookery books in the 1880s, and in her best-seller, *The Boston Cooking-School Cook Book* (1896), Fannie Merritt Farmer's recipe includes sherry and brandy, with no Madeira, and it is served on 'puff paste pointes'. She also offers recipes for shrimps and clams, both 'à la Newburg' (Newberg's spelling is uncertain). Confusingly, she also has a recipe for Lobster à la Delmonico, which has plenty of sherry but no brandy.

Thermidor was a play before it was a dish. Written by Victorien Sardou, it is a drama of four acts, set during the French Revolution and in particular the Thermidorian Reaction. This refers to the 9 Thermidor Year II (27 July 1794), the date, according to the French Republican Calendar, when radical revolutionaries such as Robespierre began to lose their power. It was the end of The Reign of Terror and the mass executions in France.

In 1891, *Thermidor* was staged for the first time at La Comédie-Française, a state-owned theatre. The dish came about at the same time. It seems probable that Sardou and his troupe of actors planned to have a celebratory dinner to mark the opening night, and so a chef named a dish to honour the event. What is debateable is the Paris restaurant where the dish was created. Was it Chez Marie? Or maybe it was at Café de Paris, and by chef Leopold Mourier; the recipe was adapted subsequently by his successor Tony Girod, who added cheese. (*Larousse Gastronomique* accepts the dish was created to honour the play, but cites its occurrence as 1894, and at Chez Marie.)

However, if Sardou and his friends were hoping for a pleasant evening of glass-chinking and back-slapping they were in for a disappointment. They had not reckoned on the admirers of Robespierre who were incensed by the play's criticism of their hero. Violent crowds arrived at the theatre in protest. Sardou's life was threatened. The police rushed in, trying to calm the crowds and deal with the disorder; there was a performance that evening, and a few more after that. But the play caused such a headache for law enforcers that within a week the show came off, and it was prevented from being performed in any of the state-run venues. Five years passed before it was performed on another of the city's stages, by which time Thermidor the dish was destined to run and run.

*

When alive, the lobster is blue. Once cooked, it is red. It is a crustacean which has blood that is blue due to the blood's high level of copper. Frozen lobster is fine; the freezing of this shellfish does not affect its quality. When buying fresh lobster, choose one with hutzpah.

Some suggest you should avoid buying a female lobster that has eggs beneath its tail, although here the usual contradictions of gastronomy arise: French connoisseurs call the egg-laden female lobster 'paquette' and consider it to be at its most delicate when the eggs are fully formed but not laid.

The execution of a lobster is also not simple. They have a complex series of brain and nerve centres, so cutting through their head doesn't necessarily kill them. Instead, put the point of a large knife through the cross on the back of the lobster's head and quickly split the head in two. Turn the lobster around and speedily split the tail in half to ensure the nerve centres are severed.

Homard à la broche is a dish which requires plunging a large (1.5 kilogram) lobster into boiling salted water for three minutes, before seasoning it and attaching it to a spit. Then it is roasted in front of a very hot fire for about 45 minutes, basting frequently with melted butter.

This brings to mind *A Book of Mediterranean Food*, in which Elizabeth David told her readers in the 1950s of roast lobsters, referring to a recipe in *Spons Household Manual* (published in the 1880s). The recipe, the great Ms David, acknowledged, 'is given merely as an illustration of the methods, both lavish and somewhat barbaric, of those days'. The recipe skips the bit about plunging the lobster.

It is:

Tie a large uncooked lobster to a long skewer, using plenty of pack-thread and attaching it firmly, for a reason presently to be stated. Tie the skewer to a spit and put the lobster down to a sharp fire. Baste with champagne, butter, pepper and salt. After a while, the shell of the animal will become tender and will crumble between the fingers. When it comes away from the body the operation of roasting is complete. Take down the lobster, skim the fat from the gravy in the dripping pan, add the juice of a Seville orange, pepper, salt, and spice and serve in a lordly dish.

In the 18th century cooks often put a skewer in the vent of the lobster's tail. No, this was not a humane form of execution. Instead, it prevented water from entering the body during the boiling process. And there was a clever technique to brighten the shell before serving: put a slab of butter in a cloth and rub the lobster with the cloth.

I do like the lobster tale in Jacques Pepin's autobiography, *The Apprentice*. The chef was making a television programme, and the plan was to film him as he hauled up cages of lobster off the shores of Long Island. He intended to cook 60 lobsters and in order to make it all happen, a couple of bushels of live lobster were bought from a fishmonger and placed in the cages. This would ensure realism. But as the cages were raised to the water's surface, Jacques writes, 'I squinted and realized that we'd forgotten to take the rubber bands off their claws'.

'The cameras,' says Jacques, 'rolled on.'

STARGAZY PIE

The world's strangest-looking pie, some of its contents emerging through the baked pastry to stare at the stars.

It is Christmastime one year in the late 1700s. Britain is struggling against starvation and in the grips of another terrible winter.

Come now to Mousehole, a harbour village close to Penzance in Cornwall. (Very much a tourist spot, these days.) The houses are being lashed and battered by the never-ceasing rain and the fierce winds of strong storms. Tom Bawcock, brave and courageous, is determined to find food for his family and the community. He gathers together a crew of equally heroic fishermen, and they make their way to the boats which are bouncing up and down on the rolling waves. Off they go. Or the others stay at home and Tom goes alone, depending on the Cornish teller of the story.

Many thought Bawcock (and his crew, if they went) would never return. That they did is not only testament to the Cornish spirit and fortitude, but wondrous because it also brought about the creation of one of the finest pies known to mankind. When they sailed back into the harbour, their boats were laden with fish. Seven types, it is said; pilchards, mackerel, ling, hake, dog fish, scad and the slender-but-tasty lances (they are sand eels but sometimes called lances because of their pointy noses).

Stargazy (or stargazey, or even starrygazy) pie is the dish created to celebrate their achievement. The star gazer is the navigator on a ship, plotting a course by the stars above.

Custom dictates that the dish is eaten in Mousehole on 23

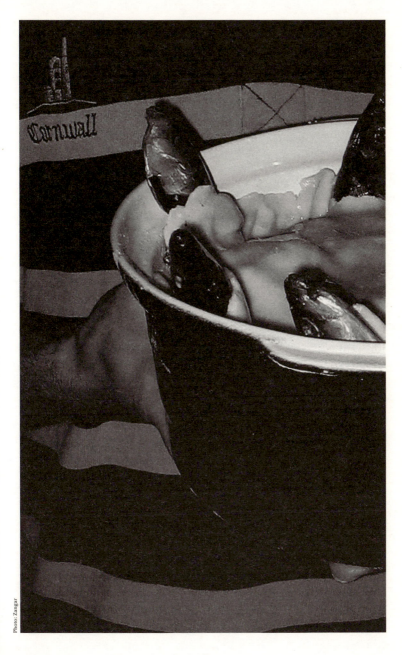

Photo: Zangar

December every year, when a festival is held to commemorate Tom Bawcock, his fishermen friends and their plight.

Through the lid of the crusty pastry lid, or around the pastry's edges, the heads of some of the fish protrude as if they are gazing up to the stars; another reason for the pie's name. Marguerite Patten was not wrong when she described stargazy as 'a most unusual looking fish pie'.

Up until the late 1600s, pastry, or paste as it was called, was not actually eaten, and was more like a 'shell' in which to keep food well stored and preserved, a sort of Tupperware box for medieval times. But by the arrival of stargazy pie, pastry was an art form, perfected by Tudor cooks, and actually eaten, along with the ingredients inside it.

Eliza Smith's book, *The Compleat Housewife or Accomplish'd Gentlewoman's Companion* (published in 1727), has many recipes for 'pye' (spelling was evolving and this was a time when soup was soop).

In Smith's book there are the usual pie suspects – lamb, chicken and veal. She also suggests a pie of neats' tongues, which are first boiled, blanched and sliced. Her battalia pye is certainly not a dish for vegetarians. 'Take four small chickens, four squab pigeons, four sucking rabbets,' it begins. 'Cut them in pieces, season them with savoury spice and lay them in the pye, with four sweetbreads sliced, with as many sheep's tongues, two shiver'd palates, two pair of lamb stones, twenty or thirty coxcombs, with savoury balls and oysters. Lay on butter, and close the pye. A Lear.' The 'pye' was closed with pastry, and the 'lear' was a sauce or gravy.

*

Traditionally, the Cornish made stargazy with pilchards, the heads left on, of course, so that the fish could stargaze.

Patten notes that pilchards have become scarce around the Cornish coast, and so for her version she suggests small herrings if pilchards are not available. First, she makes a mix of breadcrumbs, finely chopped parsley, milk, lemon zest and juice, and chopped onions. Half of this mix is used to stuff the fish; the other half fills the spaces between the fish. Next, chopped bacon and more chopped onions are added, sliced hard-boiled eggs too, along with a generous splash – and then another – of dry cider. She covers the dish with shortcrust pastry and bakes for 45 minutes in a hot oven.

Bread or breadcrumbs are usual in this pie. Some cooks add a little cream to the cider. Cornish chef Nathan Outlaw uses mackerel – minus the heads, but with the tails intact so they can emerge through the pastry – and a bit of hog's pudding, a sort of white pudding particular to Cornwall and Devon. While Mark Hix makes his luxurious version with the legs of rabbit and crayfish: 'They are both classed as vermin and in need of culling. I wanted to think of a way we could eat them.' In Hix's pie the crayfish, and not the rabbit limbs, gaze heaven-wards.

So revered is the memory of Tom Bawcock and his dish that he and it receive numerous mentions in Cornish literature. Around 1930, Robert Morton Nance wrote a poem about the pie. He set it to the tune of 'The Wedding March', a Cornish folk song. Here are a couple of verses:

A merry place, you may believe,
Was Mousehole 'pon Tom Bawcock's eve;
To be there then, who wouldn't wish,
To sup on seven sorts of fish.

As each we'd clunk as health were drunk
In bumpers brimming high.

And when up came Tom Bawcock's name,
We praised him to the sky.

Morton's odes to food include, by the way, his 'Merry Ballad to the Cornish Pastie', written in the late 1800s:

For it gives sweet ease to the scullery quean
Who hath nor platters nor knives to clean
So I wish him joy whoever he be
That first found out the Cornish Pastie.

IKA-SŌMEN

A Japanese dish of noodle-like strips of raw squid, with grated ginger and a splash of soy sauce.

Mother Nature went some way to protecting squid from predators. She made them almost translucent. They do not dwell on the sea bed, but swim close to the surface of the water. Their translucency, therefore, means they are virtually invisible to the hungry fish and sea creatures beneath them. However, there is still no protection from predators above, particularly those in fishing boats.

This cephalopod can be found in all oceans and seas, says Alan Davidson's *The Oxford Companion to Food*, except the Black Sea.

Many shy away from cooking strips of squid, fearing it will be rubbery. The trick is to cook it quickly on a high heat. It can be scored with a sharp knife, and then placed on a hot grill. If the squid releases too many juices during cooking,

then the heat is too low. Have another go. Play a song which is two minutes long. If you are still cooking the strips of squid when the song has finished, then you have cooked for too long: the squid will be rubbery.

The Japanese dish of ika-s men is even easier because you do not need a griddle, pan, heat or a song. The dish is raw, but a sharp knife is crucial.

Ika means cuttlefish, the Japanese name for squid. *Sōmen* describes wheat noodles, the width of which the strips should resemble.

It was, some say, created by squid fishermen in Northern Japan. This dish is famous and cherished in Hokkaido, the country's northernmost and second largest island, a staggeringly beautiful, tranquil place with volcanoes, national parks, lakes, hot springs and snow in the winter months.

There are disputes over whether or not this dish is sashimi. As sashimi means 'flesh pierced' then it is probably acceptable to say that it is indeed sashimi. The fillet of squid should be fresh, and is sliced to the thickness of vermicelli, or sōmen, which is about two millimetres.

The coloured outside 'skin' is removed, and the conical body of the squid is sliced once lengthways along the middle. Excess moisture is wiped away (with kitchen paper). The fillet is then sliced, lengthways, from top to bottom in thin strips. The ginger can be grated, or sliced into thin strips (slicing the peeled ginger root, also lengthways). Finally, the ginger can be placed in the bottom of the bowl, with the squid noodles on top, and a little more ginger on top.

A dipping sauce accompanies ika-s men; usually soy sauce, or mentsuyu, which is made from soy and the fish stock dashi. Ika-s men is also delicious when added to hot, cooked noodles and served with the same sauces.

PAD THAI

A national noodle dish of Thailand, perfumed with the scents of lime, garlic and coriander.

Politics created this dish. In the late 1930s, as Siam became Thailand, the government was keen to establish an identity with its new name. As part of the country's PR strategy, a cookery competition, on a national scale, was held to see who could come up with a new dish. The winner was a dish of noodles, bean sprouts, egg and peanuts, with, perhaps, some coriander. Importantly, the noodles were made from rice and not wheat.

Thailand was keen to move away from its association with China, which was engulfed in the Sino-Japanese War, and China's culinary influence on Thailand was noticeable. Thailand ate wheat noodles, introduced to the country by the Chinese. Rice noodles would enable Thailand to establish its own type of cuisine, although they could have never known just how much the winning dish would come to be enjoyed by the wider world. The noodles are called *sen lek* (small strand), or *sen jun* (jun being an abbreviation of Chantaburi, the province in which they were originally made).

There was another bonus. Thailand was desperate to boost its national coffers and rice noodles – although made from rice in the form of flour, of course – would reduce the consumption of rice. This meant, in turn, that the country could export rice and bring in a sizeable income. It took time, and there have been political blips along the way, but in 2015 Thailand was, after India, the world's second leading exporter of rice (9.8 million tonnes), with Vietnam in third place.

They called their new dish Pad Thai – fried Thai-style. And it encapsulates, and must always encapsulate, the essential criteria of a Thai dish: a balance of sweet, bitter and salty, with a creamy texture. The dish is sold from carts by street vendors, who busily feed the snack-loving locals every moment of the day. Most agree that, apart from rice noodles, the dish should contain tamarind paste, garlic, sugar, preserved turnip (also called salted radish), fish sauce, bean sprouts, prawns and egg. Peanuts are a crunchy garnish. Lime juice completes it. If you're missing an ingredient or two, do not worry.

Pad Thai is cooked in a smoky wok on a very hot flame. The soaked noodles are drained and tossed in to join the garlic, shallot, preserved turnip, tamarind paste (sour), sugar for sweetness and fish sauce for saltiness. Then the egg is stirred in, bringing creaminess, before the prawns and bean sprouts are added. Add the peanuts and give it a stir. Pad Thai is served with a wedge of lime ensuring an extra dose of that important sour element. Since its creation, this dish is cooked all around the world, albeit in versions and with ingredients which the Thais would not recognise as their national dish and might not describe as Pad Thai.

GUMBO

A bit of this and a bit of that … Family food from America's Deep South.

Abby Fisher's name may mean nothing to the American cooks of today but, in the history of gastronomic literature, she should be remembered as a great champion.

She was born a slave in South Carolina in the early 1830s. Her mother was black, her father white and French. Abby was a cook, and she married Alexander Fisher, job unknown. They lived in Mobile, Alabama, and then crossed the country after the Civil War, heading west, to California.

Abby and Alexander produced at least eleven children, but it is the creation of Abby's cookery book which ensured her culinary legacy. Once settled in San Francisco, Abby continued to work as a cook, and her talents quickly earned her a reputation and a tremendous following. At the Sacramento State Fair in 1879 she was awarded a diploma, and ladies raved about her Southern food.

Inevitably it was not long before Abby's 'lady friends and the patrons of San Francisco' encouraged her to compile a book of recipes. Doubtless, they all wanted to cook like her, although, remember, it was the slaves who toiled in the kitchens of the South who perfected Creole cuisine. Gumbo has French influences (see: Bouillabaisse) and is cooked in the iron pot much adored by the French, but it takes its name from the Caribbean word for okra, the vegetable which usually features in this stew.

However, a book would have seemed an impossible task for Abby, as she could not read nor write. Her husband was also illiterate so she could not dictate recipes to him. Maybe, therefore, she dictated to one of her kind and admiring lady friends, because in 1880 Abby's book was published: *What Mrs Fisher Knows About Old Southern Cooking … Soups, Pickles, Preserves Etc.* (In 1866 Malinda Russell – born a free woman – was the first African-American cookery book author, with *A Domestic Cook Book*.)

In the book's Introduction, Abby told readers that the 166 recipes were:

Photo: Edd Prince

based on an experience of upwards of thirty-five years in the art of cooking Soups, Gumbos, Terrapin Stews, Meat Stews, Baked and Roast Meats, Pastries, Pies and Biscuits, making Jellies, Pickles, Sauces, Ice-Creams and Jams, preserving Fruits, etc. The book will be found a complete instructor, so that a child can understand it and learn the art of cooking.

She includes those Deep South favourites such as corn fritters, fried chicken and snow pudding, and gives recipes for oyster and chicken gumbos. Then there is okra gumbo soup: a beef shank is boiled in water until the water reduces in volume by half; finely sliced okra is added – 'don't put in any ends of ochre ... Season with salt and pepper while cooking. To be sent to table with dry boiled rice. Never stir rice while boiling. Season rice always with salt when it is first put on to cook, and do not have too much water in rice while boiling.'

Oh, what folks wouldn't give for a bowl of gumbo like Abby used to make.

*

Melissa Magnuson, artist, photographer and exceptional home cook (as well as my good friend) was born and raised in Mississippi. Gumbo country. One day she made a big pot of gumbo with crab and crayfish, which she ladled onto rice in large, flat soup bowls. There was crusty sourdough bread too. We tucked in – my lord, it was gorgeous – and she told me about this dish. 'Growing up,' said Melissa, 'we were always taught "first you make a roux".' Classically, roux is the mix of butter and plain flour, combined in a saucepan over heat and used as a sauce thickener.

'The roux is roughly equal parts fat, sometimes used from fried chicken or bacon, and flour. These are cooked in a heavy pot – usually cast iron – until medium brown. Peppers, onions, celery – the holy trinity of creole cuisine – are usually added to the browned roux. These are cooked, and then hot water is slowly added.

'Chopped parsley, garlic and bay leaves are added. Gumbo is basically a wonderful way to use whatever is in the kitchen or caught that day; ham, duck, sausage – andouille – or seafood such as crayfish, shrimp [prawns to the British] or oysters, just as we're eating now. There are lots of variations. Also, we add tomato sauce or fresh tomatoes, or both.

'Gumbo can be made with either okra or filé (sassafras powder) to thicken the sauce. Filé was used by the Choctaw Indians – indigenous to Mississippi and Louisiana. Okra goes in during cooking, or filé goes in at the end when the heat is turned off.'

The gumbo debates tend to centre on which to use; okra or filé? Melissa insists: 'One or the other, never both.'

MEAT AND POULTRY

THE BURGER

A patty of minced beef which has been fried, griddled or grilled, and is usually served in a bun and with fries. Germanic cuisine meets American flare.

In 1904 the city of St Louis, Missouri, hosted a World Fair which drew huge crowds from all over America. It also attracted vendors and sales people who were keen to show off their new creations. The audience, which included a regiment of news reporters, was in for a food treat previously unseen across the States.

Foods that were said to have been 'born' at the World Fair include the club sandwich, cotton candy (candy floss to the British) and peanut butter. The ice cream cone, it is claimed, was invented at the fair – a waffle vendor saw an ice cream vendor run out of glasses, and so sandwiched ice cream between two waffles. Take it with a pinch of salt. The cone is also said to have been invented in Victorian Britain in the 1850s and, in London, Agnes Marshall gives a recipe for ice cream in a cone in her book, *Fancy Ices*. The book was published in 1894, a decade before waffles and ice cream met at the World Fair.

Meanwhile, a vendor called Anton Feuchtwanger had arrived at the fair with hundreds of paper gloves, which he gave to customers who wanted to try his steamed sausages. When he ran out of gloves, he turned to a nearby bread salesman and said: 'Can I take some of your rolls.' He put the sausages into the rolls and – in a flash! – the hot dog was invented. Well, that's the story.

Then there is the tale of Fletcher Davis, who arrived from Athens, Texas, with his new sandwich: a succulent beef patty served between two slices of bread. Thus, we have the sensational arrival of the burger which is today one of the most popular foods in the Western world. Or do we? This account has been fiercely contested, with other states battling against Texas to claim ownership of the bapped burger.

In 2007, Josh Ozersky – author of *Hamburgers: A Cultural History* and online food editor at the *Los Angeles Times* – wrote convincingly about his painstaking investigation into the numerous assertions. 'There is one contender whose claim to having invented the hamburger can truly be said to be unassailable,' he concluded. 'The sandwich we think of today as the hamburger was almost certainly invented by Walter Anderson, a Wichita, Kansas, grill cook who first made the sandwich in either 1915 or 1916.'

Ozersky said that Anderson was the first to cook standard, flat ground-beef patties on a custom griddle and to serve them on identical white buns. 'The claim is supported both by nearly contemporaneous newspaper accounts and by the fact that Anderson, with his partner, E.J. "Billy" Ingram, founded in 1921 a restaurant called White Castle, which still makes a nearly identical sandwich today.'

As it was White Castle that created America's fast-food business, he wrote, and especially the hamburger business, 'Anderson and Ingram deserve credit not just for inventing the hamburger but for inventing the culture that helped make it our national sandwich'. After all, the burger was food for the masses; a wholesome meal for just a few cents.

*

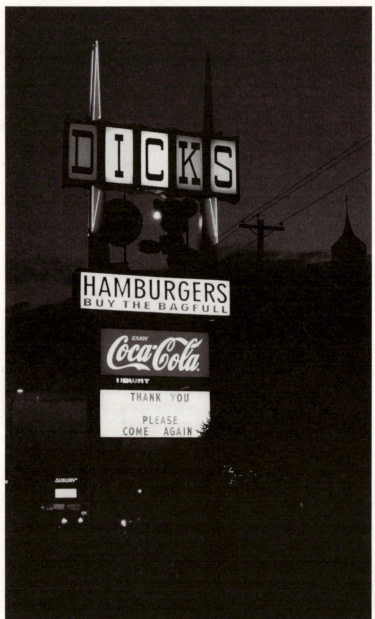

The indisputable origin of the name lies in Hamburg (the patty is not made of ham) where steaks of minced meat were enjoyed by mariners in the 19th century visiting what was then the Austro-Hungarian Empire. It was consumed not by hand but with knife and fork. From there, it travelled to America, making its way occasionally into recipe books as a 'Hamburg Steak', before becoming the innovation that fed visitors to the St Louis World Fair.

For the American cook, the Hamburg steak made a change to cooking minced beef in dishes such as meatballs or meat loaf. The Hamburg steak recipes of old are all similar. This was an inexpensive dish which did not need to be glamorised, and was simple and fast to make.

A pound (450 grams) of raw minced beef was mixed with a couple of ounces of breadcrumbs (or bread which has been soaked in milk and then squeezed dry), a couple of teaspoons of finely sliced onions, a beaten egg, and salt and pepper. Once mixed well, it was formed into round, flat 'cakes' which were dipped in flour and shallow fried in fat. Invariably, the advice was to (over-) cook them – five minutes on each side.

Apart from the regions of Hungary and the states of America, the burger was eaten in other countries, if by another name such as *keftedes* and from a different type of minced meat, be it chicken or veal.

Generally, it was unknown to the British until after the Second World War and the era which spurned a fascination in all-things American and, in particular, Hollywood-esque. Yet still, the burger took decades to catch on.

When the Hard Rock Cafe opened its doors on London's Piccadilly in 1971 it was predicted those same doors would be closing within a few months. Rita Gilligan, the longest-serving waitress at the Hard Rock, says: 'People were dismissive. They said, "Who wants to eat burgers in London!'" The cynics were soon silenced. There are still queues on the street outside, as customers patiently wait to be seated at a table, to eat a burger and drink a milkshake or beer, as the rock 'n' roll blares.

MAHBERAWI

A huge platter of many small dishes, which highlight the best of Ethiopian cuisine.

Leave behind your knife and fork, or chopsticks. The food of Ethiopia relies on the right hand and, crucially, a flatbread called *injera*, which is made from the tef (or teff) grain and leavened with sourdough. Injera is like the edible spoon. Food is collected in a piece of the spongy bread, which is then folded into a bundle and popped into the mouth.

No injera, no meal. It is an intrinsic part of the culture of Ethiopia which, with nearly 100 million inhabitants, is the world's most populated landlocked country (sharing a border with Eritrea to the north and northeast, Djibouti and Somalia to the east, Sudan and South Sudan to the west, and Kenya to the south).

Injera is the most common sight at the Ethiopian table, and is used in phrases which have absolutely nothing to do with food. For instance, 'He has no *wat* on his injera,' is an idiom for: 'He has no money.' (Wat, by the way, means stew or sauce and is also well used in the Ethiopian vocabulary.)

You do not need much money to enjoy an Ethiopian banquet. The food is inexpensive, although when presented

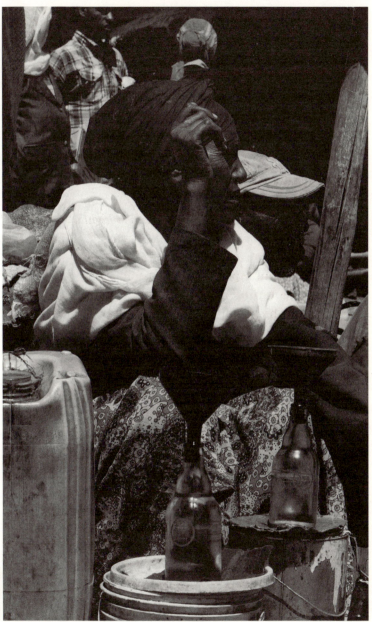

together for mahberawi it is like a banquet fit for royalty. Five, six or seven dishes are all on the one large, round platter, ready to be scooped up in that injera.

The feast might, perhaps, include beef dishes such as: *kitfo*, which is finely chopped or minced raw beef, marinated in a chilli-rich powder called *mitmita*; *k'itfo leb leb*, for which the beef mince is cooked; *gored gored*, in which beef is served in tender, raw chunks (the fat is left on) and they are either dipped into, or coated in the chilli sauce, *awaze*. *Gomen be siga* is beef cooked with collard greens, and *alicha siga wot* is a stew in which large chunks of beef, preferably on the bone, are added to fried onions and garlic; water is poured in to cover the ingredients and the whole lot simmers gently until it is time to eat.

Ginger is popular in Ethiopian cuisine and so inevitably works its way into most stews, along with cardamom and coriander, cloves and cumin. Lamb, mutton, chicken and goat are also in the diet, often in dishes which incorporate *berbere*, the nation's famous blend of spices. The Ethiopians are extremely proud of their berbere, which is a mix of dried chilli peppers, garlic, fenugreek, ginger, cinnamon, coriander seeds, nutmeg and cloves. After that, you can add what you like. These ingredients are ground up to create a powder, usually fiery both in its red colour and in its taste.

This blend features in a dish called *doro wot*: onion and garlic, both finely chopped, are fried in butter (the Ethiopians like their butter to be clarified) to become a paste; the berbere is added and stirred in; small chicken pieces – bone in – are next, followed by water to cover, and a splash of *tej* (honey wine) if handy; towards the end of cooking, hard-boiled eggs are added, their whites slightly scored to allow the sauce to penetrate.

Tibs, meanwhile, are slices of meat (lamb or beef) which have been fried in clarified butter, onions and garlic. And the spice of the mahberawi platter is tempered by a bowl of *ayeb*. This is a deeply pleasant sort of cottage cheese made from cow's milk, and sometimes used as an ingredient in dishes (fried, for instance with collard greens).

Mahberawi is very much a delight for the carnivore. The vegetarian equivalent is (*yetsom*) *beyaynetu*, which is served on the two fasting days of the week – Wednesday and Friday – and during Lent. In the vegetarian meal, the injera bread is brushed in berbere and drizzled with lemon juice, and it can be eaten with a bowl of tomato (*timatim*) salad. The wat takes a vegetarian twist when it is made with pulses or red lentils, while *shiro wat* is a most delicious vegan dish of ground chickpeas or chickpea flour, puréed tomato, onion and garlic; a healthy, spicy, curry-ish sauce and perfect on injera.

SHEPHERD'S PIE

A stew of lamb and vegetables, topped with creamy mashed potato. Piping hot comfort food to banish the bitter chill of Britain's coldest months.

On Sundays in times gone by, a joint of lamb was roasted for the family lunch after church. People went to church back then, and they did not eat the amounts we eat today, so after the family lunch there was usually meat left on the bone. And in those days, food waste was uncommon; few cooked for the bin as millions do today.

This meant that, come Monday, there was enough left-over meat to make a pie (and on Tuesday, perhaps there would be a nutritious soup made from the bone and a few vegetables). This, it seems, is the origin of shepherd's pie.

In this day and age, we differentiate between shepherd's pie and cottage pie; they are similar, but the former is made with lamb and the latter is made with beef. However, the phrase 'shepherd's pie' did not crop up until the 1870s. The pie, it would seem, was being made before it earned the name, and so was probably also called cottage pie.

The late 19th century was the age of time-saving kitchen gadgets, and along came mincing machines or, as they were often known, meat-choppers. If you were a cook and went, for instance, to Chavasse & Co ('manufacturers of English and American domestic products') in London's Oxford Street you would have entered a showroom packed with classy, novel culinary aids.

Apart from bean cutting machines and apple paring machines, there were coffee roasters, egg beaters, machines to stuff sausages, make and cut bread; others to make ice cream and shell peas. Prices for the mincing machines at Chavasse started at ten shillings and six pence, or the equivalent of £24 in 2016 money.

The mincer looked a bit like a large version of the mouli, the puréeing utensil often to be found in Italian and French kitchens, with a clamp to attach the machine to a table or counter. Like a mouli, it had a handle to turn and grind the meat. In fact, the machines usually had a wheel of sharp blades so did more of a chop than a grind, and the new invention frequently came with components for stuffing sausages.

*

The creation of the name 'shepherd's pie' leads to confusion. As shepherd's pie, the name, originates at the same time as the mincing machines, it suggests that shepherd's pie should be made with minced meat. And *The Oxford Companion to Food* does indeed define it as 'a savoury dish of minced meat'.

However, the finest shepherd's pie – the tastiest version – is made from roasted shoulder of lamb. Once roasted, the meat is 'pulled' from the bone, sliced into thick chunks and used in the pie. It is a dish of great flavours and succulence, which minced lamb cannot achieve. In other words, we are better off, I reckon, sticking with the folklore: that the pie was made from the meat of the Sunday roast. If you have not had shepherd's pie made with the meat of shoulder of lamb, then it is worth making it at home, if only just the once.

The roasting of shoulder of lamb is the easiest thing in the world.

Do not worry about weighing it or fussing with the calculation of times. Begin, simply, by scoring the fat lightly with a sharp knife. This will render the fat, allowing it to release and diminish during cooking.

Pour a tablespoon of olive oil into a roasting tin, and toss onto the oil a couple of pinches of sea salt. Place the lamb on the oil, skin-side up. You do not turn it during cooking.

Put the lamb in an oven preheated to 170°C. After 15 minutes reduce the heat to 150°C and pour into the tin 150 millilitres of cold water. This will create steam, keeping the meat succulent, and help to make the gravy. Cook for a total of four hours. Top up the water a couple of times, as it evaporates. Add a few carrots, whole, to the pan in the final hour.

Should you wish to make shepherd's pie:

Remove the roasted lamb from its shoulder. Cut the meat into quite large, thick pieces, about the length of your little finger. Put the lamb pieces into a casserole dish.

Chop up the carrots and add them, along with onion and garlic, both very finely sliced.

Photo: Joe Mabel

Use the gravy or stock (from the roasting tin) in the shepherd's pie. First, allow the gravy to cool and go cold. Second, use a spoon to scrape away the layer of fat which settles on top of the gravy. Discard the fat and pour the gravy into the casserole, over the meat. Add a little water, if necessary.

Season this delicious hotchpotch with salt and pepper to your taste. Top it with plenty of creamy, buttery mashed potato and place the pie in an oven preheated to 170°C. Wonderful smells will spread through your home, and when the mashed potato is browned to your liking the pie is ready to serve.

Shepherd's pie made with lamb mince is much improved when the mash is covered with a layer of cheddar cheese, which melts, bubbles and browns during cooking.

*

The earliest shepherd's pie – but by another name – probably originates in Scotland or the north of England where, no matter how un-tired you felt, it would be impossible to count the sheep because such a large number of them live there. But we do know for sure that the pie can only have been created after the arrival in Britain – and the British acceptance – of potatoes.

They were introduced to Britain in the 1590s. But not eaten.

The theory, as taught in schools, that Sir Walter Raleigh brought us potatoes when he returned from a voyage to America, is reckoned to be nonsense. What's more, Raleigh's name was not linked to the potato introduction until the 1800s.

It is more likely that potatoes came to us from Spain. The Spanish had discovered the potato in 1532, during their conquest of Peru; potatoes were part of the staple diet for the Incas. In fact, the Incas were the first to mash it: they dried the potatoes, mashed them and stored the dehydrated mash. Remarkably, the dried out pulp lasted for up to ten years, ensuring the tribes would never go hungry should their crops be ruined.

In Britain, as in much of Europe, the potato was generally regarded as poisonous. So for about two centuries the potato was in Britain, but was eaten mostly by experimental gardeners and pigs, fed to them (the pigs, that is) as fodder.

Authors of cookery books did not consider the potato to be food, and so did not mention it often. Even in the 1760s, the ever-dependable, pioneering Elizabeth Raffald was not particularly enamoured with the potato. In *The Experienced English Housekeeper* she found room for just one recipe, 'to scollop potatoes'. Or mash, as we know it, but browned and presented in scallop shells ...

> Boil your potatoes, then beat them fine with good cream, a lump of butter and salt, put them into scollop shells, make them smooth on top, score them with a knife, lay thin slices of butter on top of them, put them in a Dutch oven to brown before the fire. Three shells is enough for a dish.

It is best to start the potatoes on a boil, and reduce to a simmer. Maris Piper, or the Desirée variety, are good mashers.

We know that by the 1700s the stew called 'hotchpot' existed, and Sir Kenelm Digby has a recipe for it in *The Closet Opened* (1677). Hotchpot may derive from the hot pot that is used for the dish, or it refers to the hotchpotch or wide assortment of ingredients. Digby's recipe requires brisket of beef, mutton and veal, as well as cabbage, onions and carrot, and – a nice touch – a few apples (Pippins) for flavour and (as they cook) to thicken the sauce. However, the recipe does not have potatoes because they were deemed poisonous and so not even considered. Later on, the hotchpot from a county in the north-east of England was a casserole of neck of lamb, topped not with mash but with slices of potato. A bit like shepherd's pie, but what we know as Lancashire Hot Pot. That's 'hot' as in an abbreviation of hotchpot, or hot because the pot was hot.

*

Then, in the late 1700s, the history of the potato in Britain took a dramatic turn.

There was a strong push by the government to promote the tuber, and rid it, once and for all, of the dreaded slurs that it was poisonous. This promotion saw the publication, in 1795, of The Board of Agriculture's four-page pamphlet entitled, *Hints Respecting the Culture of Potatoes, and the Uses to which they are Applicable.* It was written by Sir John Sinclair, head of the agriculture board.

Interestingly, 1795 was also the year of the bread riots – violent disorders in Britain over the scarcity of provisions, mostly wheat and bread.

The lack of food was due to two reasons; first, terrible weather, including extensive floods which killed crops and livestock; second, the war against France, which restricted the importation of food. By then Britain existed on a wheat-based diet, rather than the oats, rye or barley of earlier years. The price of flour and bread shot up, and became unaffordable to the masses. A four-pound loaf of bread could cost a quarter of a labourer's weekly wages, if he could even find the bread.

So if we wonder why potatoes entered our diet in a sudden way, then perhaps the bread riots played, inadvertently, an important role. You see, as the nation struggled against famine, Sir John's pamphlet not only gave directions for planting and harvesting potatoes, but also suggested a recipe for 'excellent' potato bread. Making bread with potatoes requires far less flour than, say, a white loaf. If more people ate potatoes, less bread would need to be consumed and this would bring down the price. In short, here was a bread substitute, and anyone could grow it.

The pamphlet was despatched to the clergy, around the time the nation was recovering from the coldest January on record. With more than a hint of understandable desperation, Sir John asked for clergymen to 'encourage, as much as they can, the farmers and cottagers to plant potatoes, in order that the kingdom may experience no scarcity if the next harvest should prove either very late, or not sufficiently productive in bread corn'.

One clergyman who would have been on Sir John's side was Reverend James Woodforde. He was the man credited with the first mention in print of cottage pye. In his brilliant journal, *Diary of A Country Parson*, he constantly mentions his meals – 'dinner to-day rost loin of veal … dinner to-day breast of veal, rosted …' and so on – and his entry for 29 August 1791, announces: 'Dinner to-day. Cottage pye and rost beef.' He was not fussed about the poisonous claims and, as was customary, the dish would have been lined with mashed potato, as well as topped with it. Remember also, this was before the days of the mincing (or chopping) machine. To mince (deriving from the Old French *mincier*) was to cut into small pieces, as opposed to the modern-day practice of using a machine to create strands of meat.

Oh, to have been a guest at the parson's table. One of

Woodforde's entries notes that instead of drinking a glass of wine and another of port, he 'drank 7 or 8 wine glasses and it seemed to do me much good, being better for it'.

*

The bread rioters, meanwhile, received harsh penalties. They stole flour, and when caught, were likely to be imprisoned for six months. There behind bars, at least, they were fed: meals in jail included boiled beef – with potatoes. In Sussex, two men were found to have helped loot a flour mill. They were executed by firing squad as they knelt on their flimsy coffins. Others received the whip; sometimes 300 lashes. Others were hanged or transported to Australia, not a fate worse than starvation.

Decades later, the potato continued to have a tough fight to win us over. In 1836, G.H. Law, Lord Bishop of Bath and Wells, was campaigning for the humble potato. But he was castigated by *The Gentleman's Magazine*. 'Potatoes,' declared the publication, 'are a very uncertain crop and keep through the winter very badly. We are not, if we are wise, to trust the potato, and in particular, this potato system superseding wheaten food is, in itself, most objectionable.'

And with a whiff of Victorian snobbery, the magazine addressed its hopes for the future: 'Instead of increasing it, we hope soon to see the potato form only a pleasing variety in the dinner of an Irish peasant; and never to be found but with pork in an English cottage.'

Not to worry. The potato was by now a food of both the upper and working classes, working its way to become the most popular 19th-century street food, in baked, roasted or fried form. In Liverpool, the lamb or beef stew known as scouse, originally introduced to the city's people by visiting

Scandinavian sailors, would now incorporate chunks of potatoes, their starch content thickening the sauce so, again, no need for flour. Meanwhile, the Irish stew also called for potatoes now that they were acceptable.

Cookery books eschewed the versatility of this tuber. Eliza Acton's *Modern Cookery for Private Families* of 1845 featured four recipes alone for boiling potatoes, as well as French-inspired dishes; potatoes boulette, potatoes à la crème (in a Béchamel sauce), potatoes rissoles, and potatoes maître d'hôtel. But while she gave recipes for pies of chicken, pigeon, beefsteak and mutton, she had nothing to say of a pie with potato on its top, such as shepherd's pie.

In Acadia, the French colony in what would become Canada, they were eating *pâté à la rapure*, or grated pie, which today is commonly known as rappie pie. This dish contains 'minced' cooked meat – it could be chicken or pork or include shellfish such as mussels; there are no strict rules here. The potato is not mashed, but grated and then squeezed in a cloth to remove the excess potato water. The starch was used to do the pioneers' laundry.

Meanwhile, in France, they had *hachis Parmentier*, more like the British cottage pie and made with hachi – chopped – beef. It takes its name, along with so many other French potato dishes, from Antoine-Augustin Parmentier. He is an intriguing character from the 18th century, who did in France what Sir John Sinclair tried to do in Britain. And Parmentier also succeeded.

During the Seven Years' War, he had been captured by the Prussians and found himself holed up in prison. Now, as we have seen from the bread riots earlier, prisons were happy to serve potatoes even if others were not. Day after day, meal after meal, Parmentier was fed a diet of potatoes by his captors. You might think he would be sick of them when he was finally released but, no, he felt he had eaten extraordinarily well and discovered a fantastic new food. He became obsessed with the potato.

Royally connected, he encouraged Louis XVI and Marie Antoinette to eat them. The latter garnished her hair with purple flowers from the potato plant. Voilà! The potato became fashionable and was embraced by the French, a kiss on each cheek. But it came back to haunt the royal couple. The French Revolution – partly attributed to the shortage of bread which led to starvation – owes much to potatoes, as they helped to sustain the revolutionaries during their uprising.

BAK-KUT-TEH

Literally 'meat/pork bone tea', but tea is not among the ingredients. Pork rib and Asian spices simmered gently in a nutritious broth which is widely supped in South-east Asia.

Unquestionably this is a dish with Chinese influences, but today's version was created in Malaysia. Or was it Singapore? Both claim it's theirs, and fiercely so.

In November 2008, Malaysia set out, with some style, to prove a point. Singaporeans look away now. A bak-kut-teh carnival, lasting two days, took place in Malaysia's royal city of Klang. The highlight of the event was the creation of the world's largest bak-kut-teh.

Chefs from five of the city's bak-kut-teh restaurants gathered at a giant bowl – somewhere in between the size of a Jacuzzi and plunge pool – a metre high and the width of a tall man. The chefs then concocted the broth, the ingredients of which included 500 kilograms of pork, equivalent to five fat, ready-for-slaughter pigs. There were 50 grams of herbs and 450 litres of broth. The message was clear: Klang was the birthplace of bak-kut-teh, and this massive one was made to 'promote this cultural treasure of Klang'.

Soon afterwards Malaysia's tourism minister Dr Ng Yen Yen caused a ripple of irritation when she accused neighbouring countries of 'hijacking' Malaysia's national dishes. These dishes were, she said, bak-kut-teh, as well as chicken crab and chicken rice. Singaporeans, however, will tell you that these three are their national dishes.

The broth, it seems, was introduced to what was then Malaya in the 1930s or 40s, and by a man called Lee Boon Teh, an immigrant from China's Fujian who settled in Klang. He was a doctor, or *sinseh*, skilled in the arts of herbalism and acupuncture.

Here in Klang, Teh cooked bak-kut (from the Hokkien dialect) with its wondrous healing powers and fragrant scents. He became associated with the dish, so much so that his name was added to its name, out of respect for the creator. That is how we arrive at the Hokkien version of bak-kut-teh, where teh means Teh, and that means tea … but there is none.

There is certainly a physician's touch to the dish. The broth has medicinal qualities, with cloves, cinnamon, fennel, garlic and star anise. If handy, these can also be added: angelica root, Sichuan lovage rhizome and wolfberry fruit. Mushrooms, such as shitake, and tofu are often incorporated too. Dark soy sauce is splashed in at the beginning and more, if needed, at the last minute. Served in ceramic bowls with a side bowl of noodles or white rice, it can be breakfast, lunch or dinner. The chicken equivalent is chik-kut-teh.

Singapore's version, sold on virtually every street, is spicier (with chilli and crushed peppercorns) and lighter in colour

BAK-KUT-TEH

Photo: Chensiyuan

119

(there is little or no dark soy sauce). It also surfaced in the 1940s, stemming, it is said, from immigrants who arrived from the Chaozhou (also known as Teochew) region of China.

THE FRY-UP

A triumph of pork, with eggs, toast and condiments, and little space left on the plate. Usually eaten at breakfast-time.

'Breakfast first, business next.' So wrote William Makepeace Thackeray, the 19th-century novelist and satirist. He was thinking not of the namby-pamby Continental meal of cold croissants dipped in hot chocolate, but of the hearty and enormous British breakfast of fried eggs and fried or grilled meats, along with buttered toast smothered in marmalade. (He was, by the way, a committed gourmet and also wrote that 'dinner is for eating and not for talking'.)

At the time of Thackeray, breakfast was a relatively new affair. Go back to the medieval times and breakfast, if eaten, was only a hunk of bread. In the early 1700s, it was customary to have just two meals a day, neither of them breakfast. The first was dinner, which for the middle classes took place at about noon, followed by supper in the early evening, but before daylight faded. However, the elite upper classes had more time on their hands, and cheerfully could afford to eat for long hours by candlelight. They ate their 'dinner' in the middle of the afternoon and had a lighter meal, supper, at night-time.

Thus we have the class-division of our meals: what was known as dinner – the main meal of the day – was served by housewives to their husbands who returned from work at sixish. The earlier meal, very much one for the ladies at home, was now lunch. And supper for the middle and working classes became non-existent because they were not hungry. So in terms of etiquette, it is probably correct to call the final meal supper, but do not lose sleep over it.

Breakfast became popular in the 1700s, but it was modest compared with today's fry-up, and consisted of coffee or tea or chocolate (which was introduced to Britain in the late 1600s, and was drunk and not eaten), as well as a whig (bread roll), or toast or cake. If breakfast seemed meagre to the British, it did not matter as there was ample time to fill up later in the day on puddings, puddings and more puddings; savoury and sweet. If you had money.

*

The wholesome cooked breakfast became popular in Victorian times, and the British queen was a fan. Kate Hubbard, author of *Serving Victoria: Life in the Royal Household*, says Queen Victoria ate breakfast in a private dining room close to her bedroom in Buckingham Palace and, 'She tended to have a very protein-rich breakfast: tongue, fowl, kidneys maybe, bacon and eggs, that kind of thing.' Hubbard adds that Victoria was a gobbler, greedy and ate with speed: 'She liked her dinners to last no more than half an hour. Guests would quite often find their plates whisked away while they were still eating because once she had finished, all the plates were removed.'

It was during this period that Isabella Beeton saw the publication, in 1861, of her fantastic, phenomenal best-seller *The Book of Household Management*. Breakfast was addressed by Beeton in a serious manner, with plenty of recipes which gave heartiness to the morning meal.

Photo: Ewan-M

Beeton firmly instructed the cook of the house, in houses that could afford cooks, to rise early and begin her daily chores by setting the dough for the breakfast rolls. After sweeping and dusting the kitchen, 'the breakfast bell will most likely summon her to the parlour to "bring in" the breakfast'. The breakfast room and dining room were separate rooms within the house. The butler's duty was to bring in the breakfast 'eatables' and, assisted by the footman, wait upon the family during the meal. The job of the footman, meanwhile, was to clear the table, sweep up the crumbs (doubtless muttering under his breath about the messy master and mistress), clean the hearth and prepare a new fire. The maid-of-all-work was lumbered with the washing up, cleaning the kitchen and emptying the slops. Nice. (No wonder Beeton suggested the mistress took on some of the dusting as 'the maid-of-all-work's hands are not always in a condition to handle delicate ornaments'.)

So what did they eat for breakfast?

Admittedly many of Beeton's breakfast dishes, such as collared pig's face – the ingredients begin '1 pig's face …' – are no longer on our tables in the morning. Her breakfast recommendation for potted veal, made with minced veal, ham, mace, cayenne pepper and butter, is not the sort of dish which you would find at a greasy spoon cafe in the 21st century.

The same goes for Beeton's breakfast suggestions of potted hare, potted ham, broiled pheasant ('serve with a mushroom sauce, sauce piquant, or brown gravy in which a few game-bones and trimmings have been stewed') or collared beef, which for her was 'a very nice addition to the breakfast-table', as was potato bread when buttered and toasted. Anchovy paste was a favourite spread for toast, and anchovy butter features as a recipe for breakfast. Plain butter, she suggested, should be put in an ornamental dish, with a little water at the bottom, 'should the weather be very warm'. Savoury beef tea also receives the breakfast thumbs-up from Beeton.

However, many other recipes are familiar. There are 'broiled' (grilled) rashers of bacon ('the streaked part of the thick flank is generally the most esteemed') and broiled kidneys, as well as broiled mushrooms, piqued with a few drops of lemon juice.

*

On mushrooms, and as an aside, I recall chatting to Owen Hodgson, who briefly was a chef in the kitchens of Buckingham Palace in the early 90s. He told me: 'When we cooked The Queen's mushrooms we always added a smidgen of Marmite.' How clever! Mushrooms and Marmite are both rich in *umami*, that taste sensation found in comfort foods. This means the Queen's mushrooms were a delicious abundance of umami-ness.

Beeton gives a recipe for ham omelette, 'a delicious breakfast dish'. For boiled eggs, she says: '3 ¼ to 4 minutes will be ample time to set the white nicely'.

Her advice for storing eggs for two or three months goes like this: place the eggs in a (cabbage) net and suspend the net into a large pan of boiling water; leave the eggs in the boiling water for twenty seconds; pack them away in sawdust. Alternatively, smear them in butter or 'sweet oil' and store them in sawdust; 'the eggs should not be allowed to touch each other'.

Aside from these dishes for 'the comfortable meal called breakfast', she informs the reader of other dishes, 'broiled fish such as mackerel, whiting, herrings, dried haddock etc, mutton chops and rump-steaks, sausages, muffins …' Oh, 'and in the summer, and when they are obtainable, always have a vase of freshly-cut flowers on the breakfast-table'.

One piece of Beeton advice that is debatable; before frying sausages, she writes: 'Prick the sausages with a fork (this prevents them from bursting).' Pricking a sausage should never be done. It causes the fat to escape to the pan. Flavour and succulence will be lost. Instead, start off the sausage on a medium-high heat for just a minute, before reducing the heat to low-medium, low enough to stop the skin bursting.

Beeton, of course, did not invent these dishes, but she encouraged and helped the nation to think of breakfast as an essential meal; and an enjoyable one that would set you up for the day, providing you had the time and the money to buy the ingredients, or lived on a farm.

CHAIRO

Bolivia's wholesome soup of beef or lamb and 'freeze-dried' potatoes.

The Bolivians (producers of cacao for chocolate) are sweet toothed and they like their pastries. Inspired, no doubt, by the Spanish conquistadors of the 16th century, they enjoy a siesta after a three-course lunch and, come late afternoon, they sip black tea and nibble cakes and biscuits.

They also like suckling pig and guinea pig, and adore the *salteña*, which at first glance is almost a replica of the Cornish pasty; filled with meat and vegetables, and wrapped in pastry which is crimped along the top, or sometimes the side. Unlike the pasty, it contains hard-boiled egg, cumin and, to make it spicy, ground red pepper.

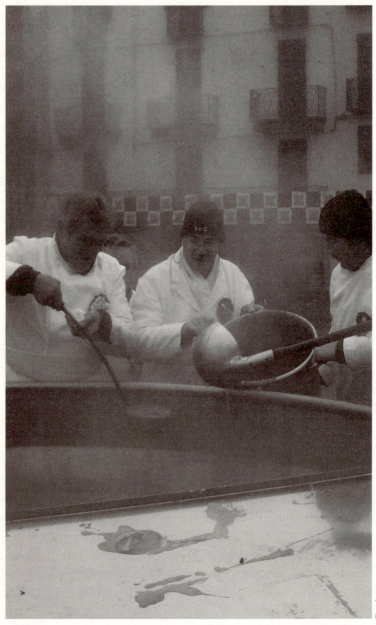

Photo: Laurom

126

The dish is not particularly old. It is credited to Juana Manuela Gorriti, the 19th-century writer, feminist and brave freedom fighter. Born in Salta, in neighbouring Argentina, she and her family decamped to Bolivia when the Argentinian dictator, the brutal Juan Manuel de Rosas, started stealing land from his subjects. Although she was not a professional cook, her pies were instantly popular with the Bolivians, and soon word spread. They became known as the empanada salteña: the pie of the woman from Salta.

Chairo is a soupy stew which dates back much further, and is eaten by the people of Aymara, a region stretching across the Andes and incorporating not only Bolivia but also Chile and Peru. Chairo is the Aymara word for soup. The centre of the region is the city of El Mato, not far from Bolivia's capital La Paz. Often it is called chairo paceño, soup of La Paz.

One large pot is required for the cooking of chairo. As well as the meat, the ingredients for this dish include chuño, which is an Aymaran invention. It is a potato which is laid on the ground so that it can freeze in the night; the following day it is left in the sun, and stamped on to press out the moisture. This process continues for a few days, after which the potato is washed and then dried to create 'white chuño'. It is an ancient technique, at least 1,000 years old, and sometimes *chuño* is described as freeze-dried potato, which makes it sound quite a modern food.

Chalona is another ingredient: a sun-dried meat, of which the technique is even more ancient, possibly dating back to Neanderthal man who was searching for ways to preserve his food. Take the meat and place it in the sun. Hey presto! It is dried and will last for ages. For centuries chalona has been made with lamb, but only because the Spaniards introduced sheep to Bolivia. Before that, the Aymarans and Incas and their predecessors dried other meats, and perhaps the flesh of birds.

It is easy to make chairo. The chuño is soaked overnight before being peeled, and washed some more. The beef and chalona are added to the pot of water and left to simmer; and then the other ingredients are added, including the chuño, beans, onion, and, perhaps, squash, red (bell) pepper and carrots. Herbs of your choice can be added, as well as the essential Aymaran herbs, *huacatay* (pronounced wak-a-tie), which has a minty flavour, and *quilquiña*, which tastes a bit like coriander, and indeed coriander can be substituted.

SPAGHETTI (OR SPAGHETTONI) ALLA CARBONARA

A classic Italian pasta dish. Cheap, quick, easy to make and even easier to eat.

This simple and inexpensive pasta dish has a name which has aroused immense intrigue. There are a number of theories of how it came to be known.

The spaghetti part of the name is fine. We all know what that is. The word itself derives from *spago*, from the Italian for string or cord, which stems from *spacus*, the Latin for twine. The pasta, of course, is like string, cord or twine. *Alla Carbonara* means in the style of the coal-worker or maker of wood charcoal. This gives us charcoal-maker's string. Easy to see why the dish has yet to appear on a restaurant menu under its English translation.

The mystery centres on the coal-worker or workers. Who the devil were they? And how and why on earth could or would they have lent their name to this dish?

One theory is that the coal-workers who slaved away in the Apennine Mountains ended their day with this dish, which was cooked on a fire made from charcoal. This theory is widely disbelieved.

Another story is that the dish was created during the Second World War. American troops in Italy had rations of eggs and bacon and these ingredients, once in the hands of the local chefs, were added to pasta to become spaghetti alla carbonara. This is not credible because the dish was eaten before the war.

There is also the claim that it takes its name from the black pepper ground onto the top of the dish, pepper resembling coal. This is also deemed to be ridiculous.

Jeremy Parzan used his website, Do Bianchi, to share his theory:

> While I have no solid evidence of this, my philological intuition leads me to believe that the innovation of carbonara was the inclusion of cured pork. To my knowledge, no gastronomer has made the connection between carbonara and carbonata, a term widely used in Renaissance Italy to denote a type of salt-cured and smoked pork.

Parzan adds: 'I'd like to propose that the designation carbonara could have been inspired by the use of salt-cured pork that had been smoked sotto carboni (by means of [wood] charcoal or embers).'

Or, moving on, it is said to be named after the groups of 19th-century secret revolutionary societies known as the Carbonari (Italian for 'charcoal makers' or 'burners'), either as a tribute to them or created by them because they were poor and had little more than pasta, cheese and pancetta, and with those humble ingredients rustled up this magnificent dish.

*

My own theory emanates from the traditions of the professional kitchens before the introduction of modern ovens. In the old days, and up until, say, the early 1950s, ovens in restaurants were fired by wood and charcoal.

The kitchen brigade was run by a head chef. The French 'regimental' or Escoffier system of a kitchen brigade is clever and still in use: beneath the head chef there is the *sous* chef, and then *chefs de partie* – chefs who are in charge of sections, ranging from Sauce–Meat, Fish, Pastry and, depending on the restaurants, sections could include Cold Starters and Hot Starters. *Commis* chefs are the assistants to the *chefs de partie*.

The phrase *chef-patron* or chef-proprietor is in frequent use these days as many chefs either own or have a sizeable stake in the restaurant. This is a relatively new phenomenon, skilfully exemplified, and perhaps pioneered, in the early 1920s by the great Fernand Point – the so-called 'father of modern gastronomy' who drank a magnum of champagne every day. His restaurant La Pyramide in Vienne, near Lyon, was regarded as the finest in France. Those who trained with Point included the mighty Paul Bocuse, another to encourage the rise of the chef-patron.

Now, in Italy, they might not have followed necessarily this regimental system in professional kitchens. Nevertheless, the Italian head chef had other chefs who worked beneath him, and every kitchen – no matter which country it is in – has always required someone to do the washing up. In large kitchens this is the job of the kitchen porter or KP.

Photo: opo le Chien

And all large kitchens required an apprentice. He would be a young lad (the girls helped at home) at the beginning of his culinary career. In return for a meagre wage, he worked long hours, slaving away as the kitchen dogsbody and learning through observation and gradual experience.

Depending on the size of the kitchen, the apprentice moved from section to section, a day here, a day there, helping out with menial tasks. At the Hotel St George in Harrogate, Yorkshire, fifteen-year-old Marco Pierre White's duties as an apprentice included running to the bookies to place bets for the chefs.

Jacques Pépin recounts his days as an apprentice in his memoir, appropriately enough entitled *The Apprentice*. Pépin's three-year apprenticeship began in 1949 at Le Grand Hotel de L'Europe, in Bourg-en-Bresse. His working day began at 8.30am and his first job was to start up the great big oven which was known, in his kitchen, as Le Piano. 'A young apprentice might never be permitted near it during service, but God help him if he failed to light proper fires in it,' writes Pépin, who adds that these repercussions did not make this his favourite job.

He was shown by his predecessor – the apprentice until Pépin's arrival – how to get the fires going. 'He let me watch while he lit paper, then wood, and finally lumps of coal in one firebox. When the blaze was roaring, he shovelled glowing coals into the next firebox and repeated the process until Le Piano was ready for Chef and the *commis*.'

So, I wonder, was this common fire-lighting role of the apprentice the inspiration behind spaghetti alla carbonara? Was this dish named not after the *maker* of wood or charcoal, but rather the *provider* of wood or charcoal – in other words, the young lad who kept the fires burning in the kitchen?

Of course, the stove's fire needed constant maintenance.

You had to keep an eye on it, top it up, stoke it and feed it. Left alone, it might die down, lose its heat and fade. The kitchen brigade found time to eat a meal in between lunch and evening service, but the apprentice was probably the one lumbered with having only a quick bite to eat in the kitchen while he watched the oven. Perhaps the apprentice had spaghetti alla carbonara by the stove, while his superiors sat in the dining room. Or maybe it was the first dish that was made by an apprentice – made correctly and the apprentice progressed up the kitchen ladder.

*

Although the origins of the dish are unknown – as is the recipe for the original version – many Italians still claim there is an authentic way of making it. Mushrooms, the Italians insist, *non deve mai essere in carbonara* (must never be in carbonara). The Italians who opened restaurants in London in the 1960s made for their guests a carbonara with bacon and cream (or a combination of milk and cream). This is considered sacrilege. British bacon is a no-no, and the addition of cream in carbonara horrifies Italians in Italy.

Chef Francesco Mazzei (see: Pizza) says: 'No cream, no pancetta. Simple as that. No one can rewrite a beautiful poem. Likewise, this dish cannot be changed. Carbonara is all about purity.' The authentic version, says Mazzei and other renowned chefs, is made with the Italian ham, *guanciale*, and the cheese, Pecorino Romano. Guanciale comes from the cheek of the pig, *guancia* being Italian for cheek.

The pasta, they say, should only ever be spaghetti or – even better – spaghettoni. Spaghettoni is thick spaghetti, and that thickness is just right for the coating of the delicious sauce.

Just before serving, egg yolks are added to the hot dish; once stirred in, a creamy richness coats the pasta, the fork, the palate, and – if you happen to drop any food – your shirt and trousers, dress, blouse and skirt.

Mazzei says:

'Sweat the guanciale in very good extra virgin olive oil until it is nice and golden. Take it out of the pan. Meanwhile, cook the pasta al dente. Take some of the pasta water and add it to the guanciale pan, and then add the pasta – you almost want to *feed* the pasta with the flavours, and the pasta will release its own starch creating a creamy emulsion with the water and fat.

'When the pasta is cooked, remove the pan from the stove, add Pecorino Romano, egg yolks and a lot of black pepper and give it a stir. It will be lovely and creamy – so there is absolutely no need for cream. Put the remaining guanciale on top, kiss your creation and serve.'

TAGINE – MOROCCO

The Moroccan take on a stew. Meat and vegetables, spices and dried fruit, cooked with just a small amount of liquid in a conical pot.

Tagine, or tajine, is named after the utensil in which it is cooked (see: **Paella**). The word stems from *ṭājin*, the Arabic for pan. It dates back to the Arab invasion and occupancy of North Africa in the 7th century (and subsequently, in waves,

over the next few centuries). Or was it a Berber creation in about the 9th century?

The distinctive clay 'pan' into which the ingredients are placed has a shallow round base with low sides.

These ingredients comprise pieces of meat – usually lamb or chicken with or without the bones left in – onions and potatoes, chickpeas, dried fruit (dates, apricots, figs), spices and herbs. Only a little water is added, and it steams the food during cooking. There are two types of tagine, and each requires a different fat and spice. 'M'qualli' is a tagine cooked in oil, and with saffron, so the sauce is yellow. 'M'hammer' is cooked with clarified butter and paprika; the sauce, therefore, is red. A cone-shaped 'lid' is put on top of the base before the tagine is placed on the dying embers of a fire, where it cooks.

In these modern days, the tagine can be cooked on the hob, using a diffuser between the gas and the bottom of the pot. Or it can be put into a slow oven.

Claudia Roden, an acknowledged authority on Moroccan cuisine, offers plenty of tagine recipes in *Arabesque*, from lamb with caramelised baby onions and pears, to knuckle of veal with bulbs of fennel.

Before cooking, the tagine pot can be immersed in cold water for a couple of hours, preventing cracks in the clay. It is also traditional, but not essential, to rub the meat with the flesh of a sliced lemon before cooking. Couscous, Morocco's national staple, often accompanies tagine. It is made from the husked and crushed semolina of un-ground wheat, introduced to Morocco by the Arabs.

Couscous takes its name either: from *kaskasa*, the Arabic word for 'pounded small'; from *keskou*, the Berber word derived from the sound steam makes as it passes through the grain; or from *kiskis*, the earthenware pot in which the couscous is cooked.

On that subject, to cook shop-bought couscous, pour the required amount of couscous into a Pyrex dish or saucepan. Sprinkle over a pinch of salt. Cover the couscous with boiling water (from the kettle) so that there is a centimetre of water above the couscous. Cover the dish or saucepan with cling film and let it steam for about five minutes.

The Tunisian tajine is unlike the Moroccan version, but similar to the Italian frittata; a stew with hard-boiled eggs and baked in a pie dish.

ROAST BEEF, YORKSHIRE PUDDING AND HORSERADISH

Crucial components of the hearty lunch enjoyed by millions of Britons on a Sunday. Pass the gravy, please.

The French term for the English – *les rosbifs* – can be regarded either as an insult or as a compliment.

As the former it suggests that, while the French are the gods of the kitchen, the British are unimaginative cooks, capable of producing nothing more complicated than roast beef. As a compliment, however, it is great praise indeed: that Frenchmen consider Britons to be masters in the culinary art of roasting, and that British beef is the finest in the world.

The British do indeed excel at roasting. This reputation long precedes the oven, taking us back to medieval times when the carcasses of huge beasts and birds – deer, swine, wild boar, sheep, capons, geese, swans and sometimes cows – were prepared for the spit.

There, in front of a blazing fire, the meat turned on the spit, cooking slowly and basted frequently to keep its succulence. The feasts of Henry VIII and his Tudor countrymen were incomplete without a roast, or ten. Venison, by the way, had to be cooked with extra skill. It could dry out easily and the meat would toughen, so a sort of jacket of pork fat was wrapped around the venison before it went on the spit.

And Queen Elizabeth, the reigning monarch, also relishes a roast lunch after church on Sundays – her beef comes from Sandringham and Balmoral. She likes the well done end-slice of the joint.

When Henri de Valbourg Misson visited Britain in the 1690s, accompanied by his journal, he was horrified by the English diet. 'I always heard,' he wrote,

> that they were great flesh-eaters, and I found it true. I have known people in England that never eat any bread, and universally they eat very little; they nibble a few crumbs while they chew meat by the whole mouthfuls … Among the middling sort of people they had ten or twelve common meats which infallibly take their turns at the tables; and two dishes are their dinners: a pudding, for instance, and a piece of roast beef.

Interestingly, it was arrival of French cuisine in the 1700s which bothered some Englishmen. They feared that this new fancy and elaborately-crafted food would lead to the demise of what they had come to savour at the table. Would roast beef, for example, become a thing of the past, replaced by posh French nosh? The committed carnivore Henry Fielding was prompted to write a song, which was set to music by the composer Richard Leveridge, and featured in the opera 'Grub Street' before the Navy embraced it as their anthem:

When mighty roast beef was the Englishman's food,
It ennobled our brains and enriched our blood.
Our soldiers were brave and our courtiers were good
Oh! the roast beef of old England,
And old English roast beef!

Our fathers of old were robust, stout, and strong,
And kept open house, with good cheer all day long,
Which made their plump tenants rejoice in this song –
Oh! the Roast Beef of old England,
And old English Roast Beef!

When good Queen Elizabeth sat on the throne,
Ere coffee, or tea, or such slip-slops were known,
The world was in terror if e'er she did frown.
Oh! The Roast Beef of old England,
And old English Roast Beef!

When the song was sung by the British Royal Navy on their ships, it was loud enough for the approaching French navy to hear les rosbifs.

Meanwhile, John Keats, one of the Romantic poets, wrote passionately of how he longed 'for some famous beauty to get down from her palfry ... and give me – a dozen or two capital roast-beef sandwiches'.

My foolproof recipe for roasting a rib of beef is unusual but recommended (if you have two ovens; one for the beef, the other for the vegetables and Yorkshire puddings):

1. Preheat the oven to 225°C (440°F/Gas 7½)
2. Weigh the beef and rub salt and butter into it. Roast in the oven for six minutes per pound (450 grams).
3. When the required cooking time is reached, turn off

Photo: Llann Wé²

the heat but leave the beef in the oven. Do not open the oven door. Leave it for two hours. Then you can open the door, because then it is done.

*

The meat had to wait a few centuries for Yorkshire pudding to join it on the plate. The pudding, which is made from a batter of milk, egg yolks and flour, seems to have been made in various parts of England. However, these puddings were cooked in a pan without fat.

In the 16th and 17th centuries, Yorkshire cooks at the spit gave the pudding a unique and individual twist with a novel technique: the batter was poured into very hot fat, causing it to rise, become crisp on the bottom and at the edges and quite light in texture. Beef dripping, arguably, provides the most flavoursome fat for this purpose and so the Yorkshire pudding seemed an ideal – but not essential – match for beef as opposed to, say, chicken or venison.

The batter was poured into the roasting tin which sat beneath the beef on the spit, therefore catching the drips as it cooked and swelled. While the meat continued to roast, the Yorkshire pudding was eaten, relished with a spoonful of jam or syrup.

In *The Cook's Oracle* of 1829, author William Kitchiner gives a recipe for what he describes as 'Yorkshire Pudding Under Roast Meat, the Gipsies' Way', and regards it as 'an especially excellent accompaniment to a sir-loin of beef, loin of veal – or any fat or juicy joint'.

His ingredients were six tablespoons of flour, three eggs, a teaspoon of salt, and a pint of milk. This is beaten to a consistency slightly thicker than pancake batter. 'Put a dish under the meat and let the drippings drop into it until it is quite hot and well-greased; then pour in the batter. When the upper side is brown and set, turn it that both sides may be brown alike; if you wish to cut firm and the pudding an inch thick, it will take two hours at a good fire.' He adds that 'the true Yorkshire pudding is about half an inch thick when done; but it is the fashion in London to make them full twice that thickness'.

*

Should you consider roast beef and Yorkshires – as well as roast potatoes – an over indulgence, then horseradish is an accompaniment of reassurance.

Horseradish is remarkably good for the health and one of those ingredients which Mother Nature provided in order to keep us well in the correct season: horseradish appears in the autumn and winter months, just in time to help ward off the flu. Which it does. (Parsnip is another seasonal blessing said to prevent a nasty cold.) You can also find horseradish in the months of spring – keep in sand or soil, ready to deal with a summer cold.

The name itself is thought to derive from Old English, when *horse* was used to signify large size, strength or coarseness.

Our ancestors ate horse mushrooms, not so common these days but delicious nevertheless and still to be found in hedgerows and forests from the middle of summer to the first frost of autumn. They discovered and named the horse mussel, also large, and still plentiful on the Scottish shores where they also know it as clabby-doo, meaning big, black mouth.

Then there is horse mint (a variety of mint, an excellent digestive and a cure for flatulence) and horse parsley, which monks grew in the well-tended gardens of their monasteries.

An alternative theory is that horseradish's name derives from the German *meerrettich*, meaning sea radish (as the Germans apparently grew it close to the sea), and that the British mispronounced it 'mare radish', which then became horseradish. But if that was the case, why not stick with 'mare radish'? I merely present the two options; take your choice. Radish is from *radix*, the Latin for root, of which there is no dispute.

In late Victorian times, horseradish cost two pennies a stick and was acknowledged as a stimulant, 'exciting to the stomach'. For centuries it had been regarded as an aid for digestion, chronic rheumatism, palsy and dropsy. 'Its principal use, however,' wrote Isabella Beeton, 'is as a condiment to promote appetite and excite the digestive organs.'

This radish, Beeton told her readers, 'is one of the most powerful excitants and antiscorbutics we have, and forms the basis of several medical preparations, in the form of wines, tinctures, and syrups'.

Do you suffer from gall stones? If so, horseradish wine may be your (reluctant) choice of drink. The wine is said to dispel gall stones, and can be made easily: slice the horseradish into cubes, and leave it to stand for a day in half a litre of wine. Alternatively, grate the radish, leave it in the wine, and then strain before consumption. Hold your nose. Drink. In terms of alcoholic drinks, this radish is more suited to cocktails, offering a welcome 'kick' when grated into a Bloody Mary, for instance.

Grated and infused with tea it becomes a drink to tackle sore throats. One tablespoon, three times a day. Add sugar and it becomes a cough syrup. It is also believed to promote the menstrual cycle.

Eating 100 grams of horseradish provides 40 per cent of the recommended daily intake of vitamin C. Flitting back to the 16th century for a moment; to when sailors made lengthy voyages, ran out of fresh food, and suffered from scurvy because of vitamin C deficiency. It is well known that, once they had identified the cause of illness, they kept limes, oranges and lemons on board. But what is less known is that at times they were also smart enough to take – and grow and harvest on board – the life-saving horseradish. In sand or soil it could be preserved for months. Brush away the sand, give the radish a quick wash and then eat it raw.

Fleets which sailed to the Spice Isles in the late 1500s may have returned with pepper and nutmeg, but they were minus men who had succumbed to scurvy. Later on, captains became more aware of the illness and stowed limes and oranges, 'scurvy cress' and horseradish. Perhaps it was mariners who came up with the idea of 'marrying' horseradish with roast beef. Cows, you see, were also kept on board ship. Before the Battle of Trafalgar, Nelson and his crew found time to devour roast beef – was it with some horseradish?

Skip forward to 1814, and the end of the Peninsular War was celebrated in Yarmouth with this feast: '... Spread out on 58 tables along the South Quay, where no fewer than 8,023 persons made an excellent repast of roast beef, plum pudding and ale'.

*

Horseradish crops up in 17th- and 18th-century recipes as an ingredient when making pickles, and in a nice buttery sauce to accompany boiled salmon or cod's head.

Turning to its preparation, which won't take long. Cut it, and note the pungent aroma: this is a root which contains glucosinolates. The same enzymes are also found in wasabi, cauliflower, cabbage and mustard seeds. This strong aroma is said to be the plant's way of protecting itself from animals and predators, which do not like the pong and so vanish sharp-ish. Many humans, meanwhile, savour the smell that clears the nasal passages and induces appetite.

Beeton writes:

This root, scraped, is always served with hot roast beef, and is used for garnishing many kinds of boiled fish. Let the horseradish remain in cold water for an hour; wash it well, and with a sharp knife scrape it into very thin shreds, commencing from the thick end of the root. Arrange some of it lightly in a small glass dish, and the remainder use for garnishing the joint: it should be placed in tufts round the border of the dish, with 1 or 2 bunches on the meat.

Quite simply, wash it, peel it and incorporate it into whipped cream. Horseradish sauce is also a marvellous accompaniment to smoked fish and superb when spread, in moderation, on to the bread for smoked salmon sandwiches.

It was the French, I believe, who improved our horseradish sauce. Originally, we grated the root and mixed it with vinegar to create a pickled sauce. In Alsace and Lorraine, and a few parts of Burgundy, the horseradish is mixed with cream before it is eaten with smoked sausages or … roast beef.

JERK PORK

Sweet, sour, spicy, crispy and Jamaican. From the pit to the oil drum, the food of slaves has become the coolest feast for the modern-day king of the barbie.

The Jamaicans trace this dish back to the Maroons. They were African slaves who in the 1650s escaped their Spanish captors and the invading British army, and fled to the mountainous interior (named after the Spanish *cimarrón*, meaning 'wild'). Deep in the Blue Mountains they had to find a way of feeding themselves. 'Jerk' was clever and sensible, a dish cooked by desperate men, women and children.

Once they had caught wild boar, they rubbed the meat in pimento (also called all-spice), which helped to preserve it. Using sharp sticks, they pierced holes in the flesh, and rubbed more pimento berries into the holes. Then the meat was wrapped in leaves. Cooking took place when the meat was buried between hot rocks, or roasted on a fire of pimento wood, but being careful to avoid too much smoke which might be spotted by the British army.

The 'runaways' developed a technique of cooking in 'a pit' in the ground. It could be easily and quickly extinguished if the smoke got out of control. The dry rub is authentic but in time it developed into a sauce – sweet, sour and spicy – that we know and love today.

Although the Maroons mastered jerk, they had learned a few tricks from the indigenous Taíno (or Arawak) tribesmen, some of whom had fled with the slaves.

The Taíno and Arawak peoples were the pioneers of the barbecue. They would tie sticks together to create a frame

Photo: Takeaway

that was waist height. They stored meat on it – it was high enough off the ground to stop rodents getting it. They called this frame *barabicu*. At some point, a fire must have been lit beside the frame and amid the sizzle and crackle of animal flesh, the barbie was born, even if the frame died.

The Taíno people had also developed a technique of drying and preserving meat. *Charqui*, an old Spanish word (stemming from Peruvian) means 'dried strips of meat'. From 'charqui' comes jerky, the dried meat, and jerk, the barbecuing of spice-rubbed meat. With their preserving technique, the Maroons would also inspire 'the rub', a term used widely by 21st-century barbecue cooks to describe the seasoning they use for meats (which tend not to be cooked in a pit but on wood or coals in barbecues made from old, split oil drums).

A large piece of meat is best for jerk pork, say four kilograms of pork loin. Pierce holes in the meat and through the fat. The dry ingredients for the sauce are sliced onions, garlic, Scotch bonnet pepper (careful, not too much), thyme, pimento (all-spice), ginger, black pepper, salt and sugar. These are mixed with white wine vinegar, orange juice, lime juice and sunflower oil. Soy sauce, or 'soya' sauce as the Jamaicans call it, is also added. It has been a popular condiment and ingredient in Jamaica ever since it was introduced by Chinese labourers who arrived on the island to build the railways. The whole lot is blitzed in a food processor or with a hand-held blender.

The sauce (which can also be used to coat chicken, lamb or goat) is then massaged into the meat, and it is left to marinate overnight in the fridge. The pork is grilled on the barbecue, ideally over charcoal of pimento wood. In an oven, roast it for two hours at 180°C. Once out of the oven, the meat should rest, loosely covered in tinfoil, for at least an hour. Pork, just like the pig it once was, likes to rest. There is also something to be said about the 'rest' before cooking: if you can bear it, marinate the pork for three days in the fridge. Many Jamaicans like to cook the pork when it is tightly wrapped in tinfoil, which is delicious but the meat will not brown or become very crispy.

GREEN CURRY

Chicken in a silky coconut sauce, hot with chilli and fragranced by lime and lemongrass. Thai cuisine epitomised.

Thailand's green curry, *gaeng khieo wan*, is not like the Indian curry. It should have the zing of fresh, cooling flavours. There must be the heat which the Thais adore. This comes courtesy of chillies, green in the case of this particular curry, which gives the sauce its vibrant colour. A spicy flavour comes from white or red peppercorns.

The curry must be sensuously aromatic, exotically perfumed by the enticing scents of South-east Asian herbs and spices. A pestle and mortar is the handy 'gadget' for grinding and combining these flavours. Fun, too.

In order to achieve the above criteria, the ingredients for the curry paste should include lemongrass, ginger, galangal (known as Thai ginger, but sweeter), kaffir lime leaves, white pepper and palm sugar. These are turned into a paste, ground by pestle and mortar, one ingredient after the other. Kaffir lime juice is incorporated, and a little water.

The curry's silky finish is provided by coconut milk and coconut cream. The result must deliver sour, salty and sweet

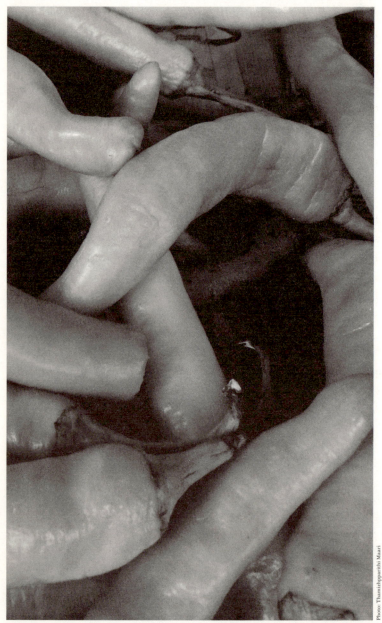

Photo: Thamizhparithi Maari

flavours to the palate, so the cook is wise to taste frequently while cooking.

It is so simple to make. In a large, deep frying or sauté pan, and on a medium heat, sauté finely sliced onion or shallot in clarified butter until they are nicely browned. Add the green chillies, finely sliced, and do not worry about removing the seeds. Stir and sauté for a minute on the same heat. Pour in the coconut milk and coconut cream, and slowly bring to the boil so that it reduces as it evaporates. Now the paste is added and stirred in.

Next, add pieces of chicken and allow them to cook on a low-medium heat. Add palm sugar and fish sauce, which is salty, both to your taste. Add whole lime leaves, whole sweet basil leaves and very finely sliced lemongrass.

At this point taste and taste again – it should be perfectly balanced. Adjust the seasoning and, if necessary, add more palm sugar or fish paste, and lime juice to adjust the acidity.

Stir in the fragrant zest of lime, again to your taste. Take a green chilli and very finely slice it, matchstick thin, lengthways; use as a garnish. Serve with white rice.

BEEF WELLINGTON

A fillet of cold, seared beef, covered in a paté and a mixture of shallots and mushrooms, and then a duvet of pastry, before it is baked. Was it named after the English duke or a street in Chicago?

There are ample twists and turns in the story of this magnificent dish, as well as a few common misconceptions.

One is that beef Wellington was created for the Duke

of Wellington, that great British general, who was born in Dublin in 1769, and died peacefully in Deal, Kent, in 1852.

It is extremely unlikely that he ever tasted the dish that bears his name. (Some say the dish – it fails miserably when overcooked – was named after his boots.)

Clarissa Dickson Wright claimed that Wellington had nothing to do with the grand old duke, and it was instead created at a hotel dinner in Wellington, New Zealand. There is no evidence to support this, and it seems all too familiar to the tale of a famous meringue dessert (see: **Pavlova**).

It has also been stated – and in the *Oxford English Dictionary*, no less – that beef Wellington did not appear (as a recipe, in print) until 1939. Apparently, this was when it was briefly mentioned in a restaurant guide published not in Britain, but in New York. 'Tenderloin of Beef Wellington,' was the title: 'Larded tenderloin of beef. Roast very rare. Allow to cool and roll into pie crust. Slice in portions and serve with sauce Madire.'

But please read on …

Most probably, the dish was inspired by France, where for centuries they have relished bœuf en croûte – beef in a crust, and that crust is pastry. Beef Wellington is very, very French. It is smothered in either pâté or foie – distinctly French products. This, in turn, is covered in a *duxelle* of mushrooms and onions – a technique of classic French cookery; the mushrooms and onions are very finely sliced and sautéed. In France, truffles are sometimes used, dotted on the foie gras.

Put simply, Wellington just does not seem like a recipe of 19th-century Britain, did not appear in any cookery books of the time, and there is actually nothing in print that connects the dish to the man, apart from the name.

*

This led me to consider the possibility that a French chef, knowing how to cook bœuf en croûte, left France and sailed off to find work in another country. As the first-known recipe appeared in America, and not in Britain, it seemed possible that this was where the chef had ended up.

And so it was that I came across Ernest Amiet. Born in France in the late 1800s or early 1900s, he left his homeland to work in the kitchens of Switzerland and England. It is not known where he worked in England, but it seems he would have probably mastered the skills of working in a hotel kitchen in Switzerland.

Amiet then made his way across the Atlantic, to Chicago and the Palmer House hotel. Today it is the Palmer House Hilton. Its history is rich in romance, charm and more than a little drama, which is worth recounting just to give you a sense of the world into which Amiet stepped. That history begins in the late 1800s with Potter Palmer, a Chicago business magnate, who married the wealthy socialite Bertha Honore, and gave her an extravagant wedding gift – namely, the hotel.

However, only thirteen days after its grand opening, the Palmer House was almost destroyed by the Great Chicago Fire. Potter, who was clearly a man of considerable resilience, borrowed a couple of million dollars and set about rebuilding it. On 8 November 1873, the new Palmer House welcomed its first guests. It marked the opening of what would become America's longest continually operating hotel.

Shortly after befriending Claude Monet in France, Bertha Palmer began decorating the Palmer House with paintings, eventually accumulating the largest collection of impressionist art outside France. The Palmer House was bedecked with garnet-draped chandeliers, Louis Comfort Tiffany masterpieces, and a breathtaking ceiling fresco by French painter Louis Pierre Rigal.

By the turn of the 20th century, the Palmer House was, without question, Chicago's place to stay. Guests and visitors included US presidents and, from Britain, Charles Dickens and Oscar Wilde.

It was an exciting place, with a heady, lively buzz, and this is where Amiet came to work, with his knowledge of French cuisine, and his experience in Europe. It is unclear when he did arrive, but his knowledge must have been extensive because, in 1929, he was the executive chef at the Palmer House, and overseeing a massive brigade. He was also Chicago president of the august society, Chefs de Cuisine Association of America. He features in a newspaper article that year, under the headline: 'Banquet often a peril, says chef.'

The report begins: 'The average American is eating himself to ill health, and if he is given to attending formal banquets and luncheons he is doing it considerably faster than if he eats most of his meals at home. That statement comes from Ernest A. Amiet …'

Amiet was quoted in the piece, saying: 'The average guest at a big banquet has a nightmare and a stomach ache after he goes home, and gets up vowing never to attend another banquet.' He was also critical of diets: 'More and more people every year are going on diets. And why? Simply because in most cases they have been overeating.'

Of course, Amiet was the chef feeding the overeaters. Glittering banquets and grand dinner functions took place every day at the Palmer House. The parties never stopped. And in 1933, the Golden Empire Dining Room of Palmer House was converted into an entertainment venue, hosting entertainers who included Frank Sinatra, Judy Garland, Ella Fitzgerald, Harry Belafonte, Louis Armstrong and Liberace.

It was all very swish and elegant, and Amiet decided to share his recipes with guests and the outside world. He wrote

The Palmer House in recent times.

The Palmer House Cook Book, subtitled *1022 Recipes for Home Use.* First published in 1933 (when Amiet was featured in the press), it was subsequently re-published in 1940. Among the recipes, it also featured 76 days of menus for breakfast, lunch and dinner. The hotel's manager, Walter L. Gregory, wrote an Introduction to the book: 'Chef Amiet has presented to the housewife a volume that can easily revolutionize her everyday table.

'These recipes, entirely new to a family, place on the home table food that will add much interest to dining at home.' People were often keen to cook at home the dishes they had eaten in hotels, noted Gregory, and Amiet's book solved that problem 'by reducing and proportioning the quantities from hotel kitchen totals to home kitchen amounts'. A cartoon of a chef's chubby-cheeked face, with a big smile and even bigger chef's hat, was splashed across the cover.

*

On page 121 of his book, Amiet suggests a dinner menu of: Petit Pain Brabantaise, Tenderloin of Beef Wellington; Cauliflower Polonaise; St Honoré cake. His recipe for beef Wellington is as follows:

> Lard 4 lbs of beef tenderloin, roast for 15 minutes, let cool and spread with cold, brown fine herb sauce. Roll out a piece of puff paste. Place the tenderloin on top and seal the meat with this dough. Paint with yellow of egg. Bake for 20 minutes in moderate oven (350°F). Serve with hot brown fine herb sauce.

His brown fine herb sauce involved frying chopped shallots and mushrooms in butter, adding white wine and letting it reduce a little; add a splash of Worcestershire sauce, parsley, chives and finish it with more butter. It is a bit like Madeira sauce, minus the Madeira. But clearly he was thinking of the home cook, the housewife, and the availability of ingredients.

Essentially, Amiet's beef Wellington was six years ahead of the beef Wellington which was mentioned in the New York restaurant guide in 1939. Therefore Amiet must take the credit for being the creator of the name. After all, he was the first to mention it in print.

But why, if the dish was named by a Frenchman in Chicago, would it bear Wellington's name? My theory is that Amiet named the dish not directly after the duke, but after the area in which he himself lived and worked. That is, the name Wellington was well known in Chicago; the city has numerous streets and avenues which are named after British places and British people.

These include: Aberdeen, Addison, Argyle, Buckingham, Byron, Cambridge, Chamberlain, Churchill, Claremont, Clifton, Cromwell, Dickens, Elgin, Hamilton, Hudson, Livingston, Montrose, Newton, Raleigh, Richmond, Shakespeare, Spencer and Stevenson. There is also a Wellington Street and Wellington Avenue which, yes, are named after the duke. And, since the early 1900s, there has been Wellington station, which is on the brown train line.

It seems entirely credible that one evening Amiet was catering for a large party of residents who lived in one of the Wellingtons, or had a link of some sort to Wellington station. What could the chef make in their honour? Bœuf en croûte, which he had eaten in France, would be perfect. But why not by another name, and one that would delight the guests?

*

In Britain, meanwhile, beef Wellington is noticeably absent before the Second World War. And, of course, it could never have been made in early peace time because of food rationing, which lasted into the 1950s.

In fact, it looks like the Wellington word spread from America; it seems they were making it first. The Americans were interested in what the French were eating, and the British were interested in what the Americans were eating.

Julia Child showed Americans how to cook unusual 'foreign' dishes, and in her 1961 book *Mastering the Art of French Cooking* she introduced excited Americans to a new cuisine (she also had a successful TV show, *The French Chef*). Beef Wellington now became fashionable in the States and then in Britain, along with those other dinner party classics of the time, coq au vin, bœuf bourguinon and chocolate mousse.

Meanwhile, in Bristol in 1971, a young chef called Keith Floyd – more than a decade away from becoming Britain's first wine-slurping celebrity chef – was serving the dish to guests at his busy forty-seater restaurant. That year's Good Food Guide reported: '... Main dishes range from moussaka at 75p or so (we have not seen the latest menu) to beef Wellington at £3 for two ... You pay 20p for cheese, but there is a fair choice ... The canned music is more obtrusive in the bar than in the restaurant. No dogs in the dining room.'

Ultimately, beef Wellington is romantic. Dhruv Baker, winner of BBC One's *MasterChef* in 2010, resorted to cooking this fantastic dish as part of his courting process when he met Aileen. 'She was coming out of being a vegetarian. I was childishly competitive, like most men, and thought I'd cook her beef Wellington. It worked!' Today they are husband and wife.

And I know of one married couple, Dominic and Romina, who competed against each other to see who could make the best Wellington. On a Saturday morning in their kitchen at home, they busily set about crafting his and hers Wellingtons. Romina cut letters out of the pastry and laid them on top of her pastry case. When it emerged from the oven, perfectly baked and smelling delicious, there was the word spelled out in egg-glazed, golden letters: 'WINNER'.

BIRDS

PEKING DUCK

The skin must be golden and as crispy as parchment, the flesh should be succulent and sweet. A treasured delicacy of China's palace tables which became beloved food for the masses.

The Chinese were the first to domesticate mallards, keeping them as pets in ancient times, mostly destined, of course, for the table.

According to *Liao Shi* (the book of China's history), roasted duck originated in the South of China. The city of Lin'an was conquered by Bayan of the Baarin in the 13th century, and when the capital relocated to Peking (now Beijing), so did the chefs who were extraordinarily skilled in the culinary art of duck roasting.

Roasted duck became a regular treat in the imperial palaces, while honey has long been an accompanying ingredient (the ancient Romans also approved of the duck–honey combination).

By the 17th century there was at least one restaurant in

Photo: Lina Ourrima

Beijing which specialised in roasted duck, although it was cooked in an unfamiliar (to us) way: the oven was filled with sorghum, the tall grass, and a fire was made. The fierce heat permeated the oven's stone walls, and remained within them. When the fire was out, the ducks went in, cooking in the heat from the walls. The birds were left with a crispy, golden skin.

As residents of Beijing developed an insatiable taste for roasted duck, more restaurants opened to cater for the demand, and an interesting development came in 1864. Yang Quanren was a street vendor who sold live poultry on the streets, but he took the opportunity to buy a fruit shop when it came up for sale. He did not want to run a shop. Instead, he turned it into a restaurant, a tiny place called Quanjude. It is said that he acquired from the imperial chefs their special recipe for roasted duck – now the masses could feast like royalty.

The ducks at Quanjude were hung from hooks in open ovens, cooking over the wood of peach or pear trees, which perfumed the poultry and, importantly, the ducks were basted all the while. Although it was small, Quanjude acquired, in time, a mighty, worldwide reputation. The restaurant was passed down through the generations, and today it is still in the family. There are ten branches, serving Quanjude Peking duck and Chinese pancakes to thousands of customers every day. At last count, the restaurants had served 140 million ducks since 1864.

Travelling gourmets, as well as the rich and famous, have often made a beeline for Quanjude. 'On arrival in China,' it is said, 'Peking duck at Quanjude should be your first meal.' In 1971, President Nixon's special envoy travelled to China for discussions that eventually led to a detente between the United States and China. During their first meeting with Chinese leaders it was a banquet featuring duck from Quanjude which helped put Kissinger and his countrymen well at ease.

Roast duck can be enjoyed in three traditional ways. First, use chopsticks to spread sweet sauce on the pancake, add a few slices of duck and slices of spring onions, cucumber or radish on the pancake; roll it up. Second, put mashed garlic and soy sauce on the duck slices, and eat in or out of a pancake. Third, dip the duck slices in sugar; again, the pancake is up to you.

In the Western world, and for many decades, Ken Hom has championed Peking duck, spreading the word via his cookery shows and cookbooks. 'I'd like to have it for my final meal,' says the Chinese-American chef. Very kindly, Ken has shared his recipe with me so that I may share it with you. It is highly recommended.

Ken Hom's Peking Duck
Serves 4–6

Ingredients

1 x 1.6–1.8 kilogram (3½–4 pound) duck, fresh or frozen, preferably Cherry Valley

For the honey syrup:
1 lemon
1.2 litres (2 pints) water
3 tablespoons honey
3 tablespoons dark soy sauce
150 millilitres (5 fluid ounces) Shaoxing rice wine or
    dry sherry

To serve:
Chinese pancakes
Spring onion, sliced like matchsticks, lengthways
6 tablespoons hoisin sauce or sweet bean sauce

If the duck is frozen, thaw it thoroughly. Rinse the duck well and blot it completely dry with kitchen paper. Insert a meat hook near the neck.

Using a sharp knife, cut the lemon into five millimetre (a quarter of an inch) slices, leaving the rind on.

Place the slices in a large pan with the rest of the honey syrup ingredients and bring the mixture to the boil. Turn the heat to low and simmer for about twenty minutes.

Using a large ladle or spoon, pour this mixture over the duck several times, as if to bathe it, until the skin of the duck is completely coated.

Hang the duck over a tray or roasting pan and leave in a cool, well-ventilated place to dry for four to five hours, or longer if possible. (If you wish to speed up the process, place it in front of a fan for several hours.) When the duck has dried, the skin should feel like parchment paper.

Preheat the oven to 240°C (475°F, gas mark 9).

Meanwhile, place the duck on a roasting rack in a roasting tin, breast side up. Pour 150 millilitres (5 fluid ounces) of water into the roasting tin. (This will prevent the fat from splattering.)

Put the duck into the oven and roast it for fifteen minutes. Turn down the heat to 180°C (350°F, gas mark 4) and continue to roast for one hour and ten minutes.

Remove the duck from the oven and let it rest for at least ten minutes before carving it.

Using a cleaver or a sharp knife, cut the skin and meat into pieces and arrange them on a warm serving platter. Serve at once with Chinese pancakes, spring onion slices, and a bowl of hoisin sauce or sweet bean sauce.

CHICKEN KIEV

A fillet of chicken breast enveloping a pocket of garlicky, herby butter; coated in breadcrumbs, shallow fried and pierced at the table. Ukrainian, French or American?

The answer to the question above is: no one has the foggiest. This is a dish of murky provenance. Where and when did it come about?

The Art of Russian Cuisine tells us: 'As the name suggests, this is a Ukranian contribution to Russian gourmet cuisine and a recent one, dating back to the early 1900s.'

Others insist it was created by the French chef, Nicolas (Francois) Appert (1749–1841). He was certainly the man who invented the bottling of food. Alternatively, it is said, chicken Kiev was conceived by the great French chef Antoine Carême.

The *Oxford Encyclopaedia of Food and Drink in America*

suggests: 'Unknown in czarist times, this dish is actually a Soviet-era innovation. During the 1970s and 1980s, it was served at the most elegant catered events in America. Eventually some American cooks substituted blue cheese for the butter or pan-fried the chicken instead of deep-frying it, variations that did justice to the original recipe.'

In Britain, Alan Davidson, in his *Oxford Companion to Food*, writes: 'It has been described by Lesley Chamberlain (1983) as "a Soviet hotel and restaurant classic", which so far as she could discover had no pre-Revolutionary history.'

The Russian Tea Room Cookbook, with recipes from the well-established restaurant in Manhattan which has served chicken Kiev since the 1940s, believes it is 'the most famous of Russian dishes' (Kiev is in Ukraine), but then admits that the 'Kievian origins are obscure'. It also pinpoints Carême as creating the dish during his days at the court of Nicolas I.

Anne Willan, author and founder of the prestigious *École de Cuisine La Varenne*, is one of many who have heard the dish was invented at the Merchants' Club in Moscow. On her website lavarenne.com, she writes with fondest memories:

I am a veteran of the heyday of chicken Kiev, London in the early 60s with beehive hairdos and skinny sheath dresses that so easily were splashed with the delicious herb and butter filling of chicken Kiev. In superior restaurants, the waiter would enquire if we wanted our crisp golden packages of deep fried chicken breast pierced in advance to avoid disaster, but I always wanted to spear my own.

COQ AU VIN

Chicken braised with red wine, bacon, mushrooms and shallots. A dish that unites the elegance and rusticity of France.

There are those who swear that only a cock (as in the male bird) can be used for this dish. However, either gender can be used, and *Larousse Gastronomique*, the French culinary bible, quotes an old recipe that uses 'a young chicken' rather than an old cock, the meat of which can be tough.

Some say it does not have a long history, and the first recipes were only published about a hundred years ago. The French, however, have for centuries been cooking chicken in wine; red, white or rosé. After all, both ingredients are abundant in France, and even the significant consumption of coq au vin has failed to put a dent in the nation's supplies either of fowl or wine. It presented itself on the Western dinner party circuit in the 1960s and 70s, notably promoted by the likes of Julia Child and Robert Carrier.

Making coq au vin is not only a joy for the cook, but anyone who happens to pass the cook's home; the harmonies of onion, garlic and red wine wafting through the cracks of windows and letter boxes. The dish is simple to make and can be cooked quickly. However, should you wish to achieve the finest coq au vin, prepare it in easy stages over three days. When you taste it on the third day you will certainly appreciate the trouble you have gone to on the first and second days.

Day one: the marinade.

In a casserole (or deep, heavy-based sauté pan), melt unsalted butter before quickly browning the chicken pieces

Photo: Gaspar Torriero

– thighs, drumsticks and breast. They need only a minute or two, just enough to colour them. Remove them from the casserole and put aside.

In the same pan, sauté diced smoked bacon or lardons. Remove the bacon from the casserole and put aside. Now, in the same pan, sauté small ('baby') onions or shallots. Again, just to brown them. Follow this by browning the mushrooms.

Once all of these ingredients have been browned and set aside, the real fun begins. Keeping the casserole on a medium-high heat, pour in a quarter of a cup of brandy. Careful – there could be flames. Keeping the pan on the heat, use a spatula to scrape away the 'glaze' at the bottom of the casserole. Voilà! The pan is deglazed.

Next, pour in one cup of red wine, bring to the boil. Add another cup, and then another until you have emptied a bottle of red wine into the casserole. Bring it to the boil, and keep it on the boil for one minute. Turn off the heat.

Add to the casserole three medium-sized bay leaves, if you have them to hand, and a few garlic cloves, finely sliced. Allow the wine to cool for ten minutes. Return the chicken, bacon, onions and mushrooms to the wine. Add a teaspoon or two of sugar. The wine will now serve as a marinade, over time tenderising the chicken and adding an appetising colour.

Day two: cooking the coq.

Heat the oven to 180°C. Place the casserole of coq au vin – lid off – into the preheated oven and leave it there for one hour. Remove the coq au vin from the oven and allow it to cool before storing it in the fridge.

Day three: heating and eating.

Preheat the oven to 140°C. Place the casserole in the oven for one hour, thickening the sauce – if necessary – with a little arrowroot. (Traditionally, the chicken's blood is added to thicken the sauce when cooked.) Taste, and season if necessary.

Once done, serve at the table while the coq au vin is hot, and with a big bowl of mashed potatoes. Finely chopped green herbs, such as parsley or chervil, can be served separately and added by guests. Warm loaves of garlic bread will certainly not be sent back to the kitchen. Red wine, of course, is essential (Châteauneuf-du-Pape).

The choice of the vin in coq au vin is a matter of personal taste and weighty discussion. Red Burgundy does not cook well: the pinot noir grape loses its character and becomes indistinguishable. An inexpensive full-bodied red wine from the south-east or south-west of France, or from Spain or Australia is ideal. To achieve the Burgundy flavours, cook the dish with one of those inexpensive wines – and then add a splash of pinot noir towards the end of cooking.

MOLE POBLANO

A Mexican celebratory dish; turkey or chicken in a dark, rich sauce of about 30 ingredients, joined by a glass of tequila or a chilled beer.

In his *International Pocket Food Book* (1980), Quentin Crewe describes mole as 'one of the world's greatest gastronomic creations'. It is the chocolate, he writes, which makes it so magical though the taste is not instantly isolated. 'In the days before blenders, a good cook would require three days' notice to make a *mole*. Now it comes in packets.'

Strictly speaking, mole is the sauce, often described inappropriately as a chilli-and-chocolate sauce, or just a chocolate sauce.

It is far more than that, and laborious to concoct. Other

Photo: Latifi

ingredients include seeds (pumpkin, aniseed, sesame), nuts (peanuts, almonds), fruits (raisins, tomatoes), spices (pepper, cloves), herbs (coriander, thyme, marjoram), onion, garlic and bread.

The time-consuming preparation involves pounding, grinding, roasting, toasting and puréeing. It is the ultimate way in which a cook can show love for those she or he is feeding. There is no room for slap-dash or impatience. The paste is diluted with water or stock to make a sauce which, in turn, is poured over large pieces of turkey (chicken is the common substitute nowadays) and baked in a clay pot. At the table, sesame seeds are sprinkled over the hot, chocolate-brown dish.

Mole stems from *mōlli*, the Nahuatal word for sauce. The dish uses ingredients indigenous to Mexico, and others introduced by the Spanish during colonisation. It is not known when chocolate was first used as ingredient. Chocolate, however, will thicken and of course colour a sauce; blood has the same effects in cuisine.

The dish requires three types of chilli: pasilla, ancho and mulato. And there are different types of mole, each of them is a dish of a sauce accompanying either meat, fish or shellfish.

Mole poblano is probably the country's most well-known and nationally-cherished dish, and is specific to the colonial city of Puebla, in East-Central Mexico. The city, by the way, is also famous for two other dishes: chiles en negada, a creamy vegetable dish adorned with red pomegranate seeds; and cemita, a substantial sandwich of meat – pork, chicken or beef – and beans and potatoes, with chilli usually working its way into the ingredients.

Mole poblano is served at baptisms, birthdays, marriages and Day of the Dead celebrations. Joy Adapon's book,

Culinary Art and Anthropology, is essential reading for mole enthusiasts, as well as curious culinary types. She writes: 'Since parties are considered incomplete without mole, and mole (poblano) is incomplete without its sprinkling of sesame seeds, to say that someone is like the sesame seeds of all moles implies that that someone is highly social and attends all parties.'

CHICKEN CURRY

Indian by birth, with Persian influences, and a special place in the heart of Britain.

Curry dates back some five thousand years at least, to settlements in Pakistan where, it has since been established, spices, including cumin and fennel, were pounded to create a powder and a paste. These, in turn, were preservatives of meat and fish, as well as flavourings, of course (see: **Jerk Pork**).

Black pepper, today the world's most commonly used spice, began to spread from its origins in Kerala. It would become one of the world's great commodities: the Egyptians shipped it for use in the mummification of bodies; the ancient Romans were great admirers of the spice.

In the 1500s the Mughal Empire stretched itself across the Indian sub-continent and into Afghanistan and with it, the dish we know as curry firmly established itself. At around the same time, colonisation brought a new but crucial ingredient when the Portuguese, having discovered the chilli pepper in the Americas, now introduced it to India. (Vindaloo is another happy result of Portuguese-Indian fusion, a hybrid of curry blending with a Portuguese meat dish.)

The Spice Routes from the East to the West would bring about curry's worldwide evolution. The Routes were held, or monopolised, first by the Portuguese, followed by the Dutch and then the British. Intriguing spices made their way back by ship to Europe and to British shores, and so an interest developed for the food known as *kari* – the Tamil word for sauce.

Hannah Glasse, the 18th-century pioneer of cuisine, was the first to write a curry recipe that was published in Britain. In *The Art of Cookery, Made Plain and Easy*, she gives instructions for 'currey; how to make the Indian way'.

'Take two small chickens, skin them,' she begins. Cut them up, stew them in water for five minutes, strain them, but keep the liquor. The chicken is then browned in a pan with butter, turmeric, ginger, onions, black pepper and salt. The ginger, pepper and turmeric 'must be beat very fine'. Give it a good stir before pouring in the liquor. Let it stew for half an hour. Then pour in a quarter of a pint (140 millilitres) of cream and the juice of two lemons, 'and serve it up'. Note her recommendation of 'small chickens'. Large chickens tend to have more fat than smaller ones. Small chickens, or better still, poussin, are ideal for chicken curry.

*

Britain's first Indian restaurant, The Hindostanee Coffee House, was opened in 1810 by one Sake Dean Mahomet (sometimes spelled Mahomed) at what was 34 George Street, off Portman Square, in London's West End. A green plaque marks the spot, or is close enough to the original site.

Mahomet placed an advertisement in *The Times*, announcing to readers that he had fitted up the property:

… Neatly and elegantly, for the entertainment of Indian gentlemen, where they may enjoy the Hoakha, with real Chilm tobacco, and India dishes, in the highest perfection, and allowed by the greatest epicures to be unequalled to any curries ever made in England with choice wines, and every accommodation, and now looks up to them for their future patronage and support, and gratefully acknowledges himself indebted for their former favours, and trusts it will merit the highest satisfaction when made known to the public. [Suggested further reading: *The Hindostanee Coffee House* by Colin Bannon.]

Queen Victoria's love of Indian food helped enormously to establish the British love of curry and, apart from a blip here and there, the passion for the spicy food has continued. After the Second World War Indian restaurants started to pop up, occupying the sites of bombed out fish and chip shops, although curry was often served as an additional meal to the fish and chips. The 1960s and 70s also saw an influx of Bangladeshi immigrants, which encouraged the opening of more restaurants. There are an estimated 10,000 Indian restaurants in Britain today.

Interestingly however, they are now on the decline, and for a number of reasons.

Firstly there is greater availability and variety of other types of cuisine, many of which deliver a cheaper meal. Most Indian restaurants in Britain are family-run businesses, and the younger generations, after studying at university, look for jobs away from the kitchen or dining room, perhaps in the medical or legal professions. Restaurateurs frequently complain that they cannot find good chefs. Meanwhile, the weakness of the British pound has also led to increased food costs. Indian restaurants have always been places for the

evening crowd, and have struggled to find lunchtime trade. In short, costs are rising and profits are falling.

This does not mean that fewer Indian meals are consumed. Indian ready meals line the shelves of supermarkets – it can be more convenient to cook a meal at home than eat one in a restaurant. And there may be fewer Indian restaurants, but the curry is still being relished on every British high street: the most successful curry vendor is J.D. Wetherspoons, the pub chain.

Here are some of the most popular curries in Britain …

Balti: stemming from the word 'bucket', this is a style of cooking in a balti pan which is deep, and looks a bit like a Chinese wok. The balti is a famous dish in Northern Pakistan.

Bhuna: spices are toasted or fried, before meat is added.

Biryani: originally, rice and meat baked together, but spiced up by the cooks of Moghul emperors.

Dhansak: *dhan* means rice and *sak* is the sauce of beans or pulses and vegetables. Lentils (dhal) should feature.

Dopiaza: literally, double onions. The first lot are fried with spices to a melting mass before the meat is added, while the second lot are lightly fried or tossed in raw towards the end of cooking.

Jalfrezi: 'hot fry' because this is a bit of a stir-fry, with green chillies an essential ingredient.

Korma: onions, curry powder and spices are fried in

ghee, and the sauce is thickened by coconut milk and coconut cream. Medium.

Madras: a hot curry, more of an Anglo-Indian creation than a traditional Indian dish.

Pasanda: from the Urdu 'favourite' because the favourite cut of the meat is used, traditionally a leg of lamb, which is marinated in yoghurt and spices before it is braised with onions, cumin and other spices.

Rogan Josh: rogan is fat and josh means intense, giving us intense fat, or bubbling fat (which is ghee). This Kashmir dish, therefore, is cooked quickly and on a high heat – pieces of lamb braised in the pans with ingredients that include red chillies.

Vindaloo: Goan and extremely hot.

*

Diane Sequeira makes one of the finest home-cooked curries I have ever tasted. So good, in fact, that it would be rude not to share the recipe, which she has kindly given to me. Diane is not a chef, but the mother of my friend, Giles. Clearly, he was exceptionally well fed as a child.

Often the onions are undercooked in curry. Here, Diane sautés them for ten minutes. Also, the curry simmers for an hour, softening the heat of the spices. The spices should come at the start, and not at the end. Diane serves her curry with basmati rice and raita, the cooling yoghurt-cucumber accompaniment to mellow the heat of the curry.

'It is such a simple recipe, made up with basic ingredients,' says Diane. 'However, the "deliciousness" must emanate from the love that goes into the preparation and the appreciation from the recipients helps, as well.'

Notes: washing rice before cooking removes the starch, so the grains won't stick together. When the chicken has been simmering for fifteen or twenty minutes, start to cook the rice.

If you want more heat to the curry, add one or two teaspoons of curry powder to the sauce at stage two.

Diane Sequeira's Chicken Curry
Serves 4–6

Ingredients

For the curry:

1 chicken (or 2 poussin), cut into pieces (if buying the chicken in pieces; 2 thighs, 2 drumsticks, 2 wings, 2 breasts, cut in half)
2 tablespoons olive oil
1 onion, finely sliced in rings
1 green chilli, sliced lengthways and then in half
2 garlic cloves, peeled and finely sliced
½ thumb-sized piece of fresh root ginger, peeled, finely sliced and diced
1 tablespoon rogan josh paste (*Patak's* is good)
½ teaspoon ground coriander
½ teaspoon ground cumin powder
½ teaspoon turmeric
½ tin chopped tomatoes
1 teaspoon malt vinegar

For the rice:

2 mugs basmati rice
1 onion, finely sliced in rings
1 roasted cardamom
½ stick cinnamon
1 bay leaf
¼ teaspoon saffron powder
1 cup mixed frozen vegetables (carrots, peas, sweetcorn)
1 chicken stock cube

For the raita:

250 grams Greek yoghurt
½ onion, ½ carrot, ¼ cucumber; all peeled and finely
    sliced
½ teaspoon ground coriander
½ teaspoon cumin
½ handful fresh mint, finely chopped (optional)
Salt to taste

In a large saucepan, heat the olive oil. Add the onions and sauté for about ten minutes, stirring occasionally, until translucent. Don't let them burn!

Add the green chilli, garlic, ginger, coriander, cumin, turmeric, rogan josh paste, tomatoes and vinegar. Add 300 millilitres hot water and stir well.

Place the chicken into the pan.

Bring to the boil, turn down the heat. Place a lid on the pan.

Continue to cook, but on a low heat.

Allow to simmer gently for about 50–60 minutes. To check the chicken is cooked, remove a piece and cut into it.

Wash and drain the rice three times in a large bowl of cold water.

In a large saucepan, heat the olive oil. When it is hot, add the onion and sauté until brown.
Add the rice, stir well and cook for two minutes. Add all the other ingredients, stir well. Pour in two mugs hot water. Place a lid on the pan and bring to the boil.

Once it has boiled, immediately reduce heat to low, and cook for about fifteen minutes (or follow cooking instructions on rice packet).

To make the raita: combine all the ingredients. Before serving, garnish the raita with tomatoes and fresh coriander.

ROASTED WOODCOCK

A little bird, these days sadly missing from many British tables.

The woodcock is a wading bird with a large beak, and is in season from November to February. Isabella Beeton, in her *Household Management* of 1861, provides an interesting overview and insight, writing that this small bird '... being migratory in its habits, has, consequently, no settled habitation; it cannot be considered as the property of any one, and is, therefore, not game by law'.

> It breeds in high northern latitudes, and the time of its appearance and disappearance in Sweden coincides exactly with that of its arrival in and return from Great Britain. On the coast of Suffolk its vernal and autumnal visits have been accurately observed. In the first week of October it makes its appearance in small numbers, but in November and December it appears in larger numbers, and always after sunset, and most gregariously. In the same manner as woodcocks take their leave of us, they quit France, Germany, and Italy, making the northern and colder climates their summer rendezvous …

In the latter part of October, writes the Victorian cook, woodcocks visit Burgundy but only for a few weeks, 'the country being hard, and unable to supply them with such sustenance as they require'.

She continues:

> In the winter, woodcocks are found as far south as Smyrna and Aleppo, and, during the same season, in Barbary, where the Africans name them 'the ass of the partridge.' It has been asserted that they have been seen as far south as Egypt, which is the most remote region to which they can be traced on that side of the eastern world; on the other side, they are common in Japan.

Beeton adds that the flesh of the woodcock 'is held in high estimation; hence the bird is eagerly sought after by the sportsman … These are most delicious birds when well

Photo: Fyn Kynd

cooked, but they should not be kept too long: when the feathers drop, or easily come out, they are fit for table.'

The bird's organs are an essential part of this feast. Or, as Beeton points out, the woodcocks 'should not be drawn, as the trails are, by epicures, considered a great delicacy'.

Her recipe is as follows …

Pluck, and wipe them well outside; truss them with the legs close to the body, and the feet pressing upon the thighs; skin the neck and head, and bring the beak round under the wing. Place some slices of toast in the dripping-pan to catch the trails, allowing a piece of toast for each bird. Roast before a clear fire from 15 to 25 minutes; keep them well basted, and flour and froth them nicely. When done, dish the pieces of toast with the birds upon them, and pour round a very little gravy; send some more to table in a tureen.

On one occasion I had the pleasure of eating woodcock, cooked by Marco Pierre White (while working on *Essentially Marco*).

He smeared a couple of the birds with clarified butter and popped them onto a roasting tin and this onto the top shelf of an oven, preheated to 200°C. There they stayed for about twelve or fifteen minutes before they were removed from the oven. The birds were left to 'rest' for five minutes, before Marco used a teaspoon to remove the intestines, hearts, livers and gizzards. The gizzards were discarded. The rest was chopped up to become a smooth paste which, in turn, was mixed with an equal amount of foie gras (chicken liver can be used instead) and very finely sliced shallot. 'That,' said Marco, 'is the most amazing game paté you'll ever taste,' and he was not wrong.

Under a hot grill he flashed wild mushrooms – only for a minute or so – and then toasted the white bread, crusts removed. The toast was buttered, and then smothered with the paté. Again this went under the grill for just under a minute. With a kitchen knife, he split the birds' heads down the middle and propped the roasted woodcocks, with their heads, on the toast. He served them in a large iron pan. The whole thing was cooked in about twenty minutes, start to finish, and certainly did not take long to be eaten.

VEGETARIAN

GAZPACHO

A cold, refreshing soup to cool down the Spanish on a hot day.

Nowadays this soup is made with tomatoes and, indeed, we tend to think of it as a chilled tomato soup. Gazpacho was conceived, however, before tomatoes were even known to the Spanish. In its earliest form, it was introduced by the Moors during their occupation of Spain in the 8th and 13th centuries.

The name of the soup derives from the Spanish *caspicias*, meaning remnants (because left-overs were the ingredients for this dish). Or it stems from the Mozarabic *gazpelago* from Latin *gazophylacium*, meaning 'treasure-chest in a church' (like a pie, there are lots of interesting ingredients). What about the theory that the word stems from *gazaz*, a Hebrew word meaning 'to break into pieces'?

Caspicias, gazpelaǧo or gazaz, the choice is yours. (Meanwhile gazpachuelo is a different soup, served in the city of Malaga, and made not primarily with vegetables but with seafood such as clams, and served hot in winter, with a dollop of mayonnaise on top.)

Even if we are unsure of the name, we do know that the first recipes contained heaps of garlic and olive oil, of course, along with salt and water, and bread. Vinegar was an essential addition, bringing extra depth of refreshment to the palate (the Romans used vinegar in their soups). The ingredients were pounded together in a mortar to produce the soup. Perhaps more water was then added, depending on the consistency. Farmers and labourers, who were not in the kitchen but out in the fields, could make the soup in *un dornillo*, a large, wooden bowl.

Some cooks still favour the mortar as the utensil in which to make this dish. The tomatoes should be ripe and sweet, and sieved to remove the seeds. The bread is best when hard, say a week old. Sherry or Jerez vinegar is the vinegar to use, and it is not uncommon to add just a splash of sherry too. Why not?

Before the Arabian arrival, the Spanish had for centuries enjoyed bowls of sopa de ajo (garlic soup) which, again, was pounded in the mortar, and sopa de alamendras (almond soup) made in the same way and eagerly adopted by the British as an 'allowable' dish to eat when fasting and avoiding meat. Sometimes the two are united: almonds, along with garlic, are used in ajo blanco, which can be adorned with grapes or watermelon.

*

Christopher Columbus, it is said, came across the tomato in 1493, during his voyage of the Americas. The Spanish conquistador Hernán Cortés, it is also said, discovered the tomato in the Aztec city of Tenochtítlan, before taking tomato seeds back to Europe. Once in Spain, it was certainly grown there, but not necessarily eaten by many people. As in Italy and Britain, the tomato was deemed to be poisonous. The Italians preferred it as a table decoration, and so a craze began in other parts of Europe.

New foods were often considered poisonous until they became fashionable, at which point they were hailed as an aphrodisiac. Hence the passionate embrace of the tomato as an apple of love: the French called it pomme d'amour, the Italians christened it pomodoro. It is likely that most of the tomatoes were orange rather than red, so could have also been *apples of gold*. The British, meanwhile, stayed close to the Spanish tomate which, in turn, comes from *tomatl*, the Aztec's word for 'the plump fruit' or 'the swelling fruit'. Although often treated as a vegetable for culinary purposes, the tomato is, by scientific definition, a fruit as its seeds are to be found within its skin.

The tomato was being grown in Britain in 1554 by Patrick Bellow, but possibly not to eat. Queen Elizabeth I was one of many who thought that the tomato, because of its vibrant colour, was poisonous. John Gerrard, in *The Herball or Generall Historie of Plantes* (1597) decreed with authority that the plant was 'of ranke and stinking savour', and when, in the 1660s, the British horticulturalist John Ray visited Italy he was alarmed to see Italians eating a tomato sauce, which included marrows, salt and oil. He concluded with confidence that tomatoes, when cooked in oil, could be a cure for scabies – they should not be consumed, of course, but rubbed on the irritated skin.

The earliest known printed recipe with tomatoes came in the Italian cookbook, *Lo scalca alla moderna* (The Modern

Steward), written by Antonio Latini, an extravagantly-bewigged Neapolitan who was skilled in cookery and stewardship, was good with a sword and had also been a wardrobe attendant.

His book was published in two volumes (1692 and 1694) and gives a recipe for 'salsa di pomodoro alla spagnuola' – tomato sauce, Spanish style. Interestingly, the sauce is what now we might not consider to be Spanish, but rather a typical Italian tomato sauce, or Napoli sauce; the type we would serve on pasta.

> Take half a dozen ripe tomatoes and roast them in embers, and when they are charred, carefully remove the skin, and mince them finely with a knife; add as many onions, finely minced, as desired; chillies, also finely minced; and a little quantity of thyme. After mixing everything together, add a bit of salt, oil and vinegar, and it will be a very tasty sauce, for boiled dishes or anything else.

Lest there be any doubt about the origin of tomato sauce (and a spicy one at that), the award should probably go to the Aztecs, whose diet included a sauce of tomatoes and pumpkins, with chilli peppers added.

By the 1750s a few Italian chefs were championing the tomato, although still advising their quivering audience that the poisonous skin and seeds should be removed before cooking. Brave monks in monasteries and courageous nuns in convents grew tomatoes, and were starting to realise the fruit could be eaten. Ever so slowly, the tomato was moving in the plant listings from 'ornament' to … 'vegetable'.

It was not until 1745 that tomatoes truly triumphed in a cookery book, when Juan Altamiras gave as many as thirteen recipes with tomato as an ingredient.

*

The gazpacho that we know today originated in the 1800s as 'Andalusian gazpacho'. That is when the French emperor Napoleon III married Eugenia de Montijo of Granada. The emperor not only had a Spanish wife to love, but he also discovered the Spanish dishes that she loved, and could cook (or instruct her cooks to cook). One of these dishes was gazpacho, and now it would become known in France, even if it was still unknown in northern Spain.

And so the tomato worked its way into Spanish cuisine, and into the gazpacho of Andalusia. Along came accompaniments to the cold dish – sliced cucumber, perhaps because of its refreshing, cooling qualities, and red (bell) pepper. Garlic must be used, as it was in the Moor-ish original. And bread was and is still involved, either placed in the bowl before the soup is poured over it, or served on the side, or even as croutons or small squares of toast.

A recipe for gazpacho – 'gaspacha Spanish' – is given by the American Mary Randolph in her 1824 classic, *The Virginia Housewife: or, Methodical Cook*. Randolph's sister had lived in Spain and was, therefore, a source of Spanish recipes, which included *ropa vieja*: ripened, skinned tomatoes fried with shreds of 'cold meat of fowl'.

Here is Randolph's recipe for the 19th-century gazpacho:

Put some soft biscuit or toasted bread in the bottom of a sallad bowl, put in a layer of sliced tomatos with the skin taken off, and one of sliced cucumbers, sprinkled with pepper, salt, and chopped onion; do this until the bowl is full, stew some tomatos quite soft, strain the juice, mix in some mustard and oil, and pour over it; make it two hours before it is eaten.

She was something of a culinary crusader, considering the bizarre events of 1820, just four years before the publication of her book. It was then that Colonel Robert Johnson, a horticulturalist and farmer from Salem, New Jersey, astonished townsfolk when, before a large crowd, he devoured an entire tomato to prove that it was not poisonous. He had announced that he would eat the fruit – also called the wolf peach, Jerusalem apple or love apple – on the steps of the county courthouse at noon. This is from *The Story of Robert Gibbon Johnson and the Tomato,* by The Salem County Historical Society:

> That morning, in 1820, about 2,000 people were jammed into the town square ... The spectators began to hoot and jeer. Then, 15 minutes later, Col. Johnson emerged from his mansion and headed up Market Street towards the Courthouse. The crowd cheered. The firemen's band struck up a lively tune. He was a very impressive-looking man as he walked along the street. He was dressed in his usual black suit with white ruffles, black shoes and gloves, tricorn hat, and cane.

'At the Court House steps he spoke to the crowd about the history of the tomato ... He picked a choice one from a basket on the steps and held it up so that it glistened in the sun.' At this point, he announced to the crowd: 'To help dispel the tall tales, the fantastic fables that you have been hearing ... And to prove to you that it is not poisonous I am going to eat one right now.'

The audience, jaws on the dusty ground, watched, and:

… There was not a sound as the Colonel dramatically brought the tomato to his lips and took a bite. A woman in the crowd screamed and fainted but no one paid her any attention; they were all watching Col. Johnson as he took one bite after another … He raised both his arms, and again bit into one and then another. The crowd cheered and the firemen's band blared a song.

The crowd shouted: 'He's done it. He's still alive.'
Johnson did indeed die, but 30 years later.

KÄSKNÖPFLE

Comfort dish extraordinaire to rival mac 'n' cheese. Miniature noodles coated in cheese, savoured beside a log fire while gazing at the snowy peaks of Liechtenstein.

Once a billionaires' tax haven, the Principality of Liechtenstein is a German-speaking micro-state, and a land of fairy tale charm and alpine beauty. The country borders Switzerland to the south and west, and Austria to the east and north. Indeed, the entire western border is formed by the Rhine river. A landscape of forests is dotted with medieval castles and snow-draped mountains.

Liechtenstein is small. It has one hospital (in Vaduz, the capital) and no airport (should you wish to visit by air, take a flight to Zurich). The police force comprises 125 officers. The army was disbanded in 1868, following the Austro-Prussian War, during which 80 soldiers went off to fight. None of them ended up fighting and so, thankfully, there were no national fatalities on the fields of conflict. The country has a population of 37,000, less than half the capacity of Wembley Stadium.

Time, it seems, has stood still in Liechtenstein, which is just the way they like it. They will never run out of booze. There are a couple of breweries, as well as the Telsington whisky distillery, and wine producers include The Prince of Liechtenstein Winery which has the four-hectare Herawingert vineyards in Vaduz and is open to visitors. It has south-west facing slopes, good soil and the grapes are helped along by the warm *föhn* wind. The pinot noir and chardonnay grapes grow exceptionally well here.

Food slips its way neatly into the country's fables. There is, for instance, the legend of the three sisters who, on the Feast of the Assumption, left their village and set off to pick berries. As they walked along the path they heard the peal of church bells, announcing the holy feast and calling worshippers to church. One of the sisters suggested they should head back, but the other two replied that the baskets had to be full of berries. They continued to pick, and filled their baskets. On their way home they met a beautiful woman who asked them for some berries. The sisters were reluctant to give her any: 'If you want berries pick them yourself.'

Suddenly, a halo appeared above the woman's head. 'You have dishonoured my holy day,' she told the terrified children, 'by not giving me what I asked for. Your hearts are made of stone. So you shall be turned to stone and remain here forever.' In a flash the sisters were transformed into huge rocks. There they remain to this day: the *Drei Schwestern* (Three Sisters) is a trio of rugged peaks on a mountain chain high above the village of Planken.

*

You can easily imagine what they like to eat in Liechtenstein. Hearty, nutritious, warming, filling food, with neighbourly influences from Austria and Switzerland. Deer is plentiful, and favourite dishes include jugged venison. Smoked pork and sausages are part of the daily diet, and rösti, the Swiss dish of fried, grated potatoes is prominent too, as is the ham-and-dumpling broth, *hafalaab*.

Then there is a sort of porridge, traditionally a peasant's breakfast (lunch and dinner), called *ribel* or *rebl*. For this, cornmeal is simmered in milk and water, before the thickened mixture is fried gently in butter on a low heat. It is eaten with compotes of apple or cherry, or both.

No Liechtenstein feast is complete, however, without käsknöpfle, cheesy noodles. This is by far the most cherished national dish, similar to spätzle with cheese, which is enjoyed in nearby Bavaria, Switzerland and Hungary.

Käs is cheese and *knöpfle* means (small) buttons which, in this case, are made from dough. The dough is pushed through a device called a *knöpflehobel* (or *spätzlehobel*): a button planer. This device has small holes and, as the dough passes through them, little 'buttons' of noodles are created. A colander can be used if the holes are large, but is messier than the knöpflehobel. Pushing the dough through the dull side of a cheese grater also works.

The dough-pushing takes place over a big pot of boiling water, so that the buttons fall into the bubbling hot liquid. First, they sink. Second, they rise, at which point they are cooked and can be lifted from the water with a skimmer or slotted spoon. The knöpfle are covered in grated cheese, given a stir, and then served with onions, which have been sliced and fried in butter to a crisp. A pot of apple compote and a glass of chilled chardonnay are pleasant accompaniments.

The recipe follows:

Serves 4

Ingredients

For the dough:
300 grams flour
4 eggs
250 millilitres fresh water
a pinch or two each of pepper, nutmeg and salt

For the cheese:
200 grams Appenzeller or Gruyère or Emmental (also
   known as Emmentalier)
100 grams Fontina

Fry some onion rings in butter until they are golden, and put to one side.

In a large bowl, mix the dough ingredients. Cover with a tea towel, and leave for 30 minutes.

In a large saucepan, bring well-salted water to a rapid boil.

Pass the dough through the knöpflehobel (or dull side of a cheese grater) into the water. As the 'buttons' rise to the water's surface, remove them and place them in a bowl. Quickly add the cheese. Toss and stir.

Place the onions on a high heat for only a minute or so, and spoon them on top of the käsknöpfle. Serve.

ASPARAGUS, POACHED EGG, HOLLANDAISE SAUCE

Purity on a plate. Typically enjoyed in Britain and France.

What came to Britain first; the chicken or the egg? Both arrived simultaneously, during the Iron Age, and were brought by migrating tribes. That is the accepted theory, and little more is known. The birds were not eaten, it seems, but bred for fighting. Their eggs, too, would have to wait to see a plate. The Romans, arriving in Britain in the 1st century, came with cargos of chicken and eggs – both of which they ate with enthusiastic vigour. And both would work their way into the British diet, and then some.

Today the British eat 10 million eggs every day. Of chickens, The Poultry Site reports: 'Around 95 per cent of the population eat chicken, and they tend to do so at least twice a week. Over the course of a year that's 6.3 billion occasions where chicken is eaten in homes, schools, hospitals, and restaurants across the country.' (The people of Hong Kong, by the way, are the world's greatest consumers of chicken.)

As with the ancient Greeks and Egyptians, the Romans were fans of asparagus and introduced the vegetable to Britain, although it took many centuries to establish itself as a popular vegetable. The Roman cook Apicius had a recipe for what we might know today as asparagus omelette. The asparagus is pounded in a mortar with wine, passed through a sieve, and then fried in a pan with black pepper, coriander, lovage, onion, the herb savory, more wine, liquamen and olive oil. Eggs are then poured into the pan, and the whole lot cooks on the fire until set.

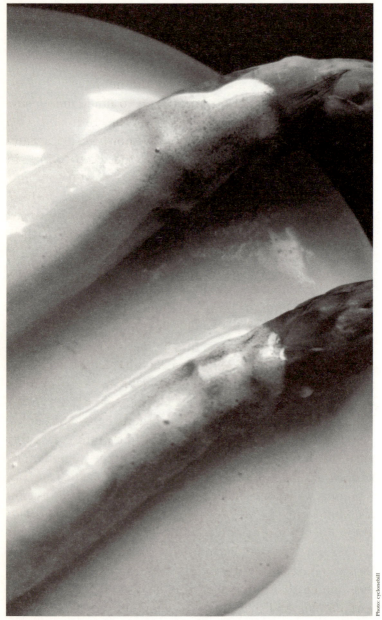

Photo: cyclonebill

In 15th-century Italy, the fabled gourmet Bartolomeo Platina viewed asparagus as a delicacy of princes, and declared that it was beneficial for the intestines, eyes, stomach and kidneys, and 'excites lechery'.

Medieval Britain, it must be said, did not have a taste for asparagus. The vegetable only began to enter the cuisine of Britain, Germany and France in the 16th and 17th centuries. In Britain it was commonly known as sperage and then sparrow grass; asparagus became the accepted form in the 19th century.

The diarist Samuel Pepys mentions a shopping trip in 1667, from which, '… Brought home with me from Fenchurch St a hundred of sparrow grass, cost 18d'. He was buying in April, right at the beginning of the asparagus season, which is said to begin officially on St George's Day, 23 April. Pepys' journal shows that he beat that by two days. (Asparagus from the Wye Valley, on the border of England and Wales, is often said to be the best in Britain.)

In France, Louis XIV had asparagus 'force' grown in hothouse beds within greenhouses at the Palace of Versailles, enabling him to eat it for most of the year. The French would come to enjoy the asparagus–egg pairing. In Lorraine (home of the quiche) and Franche-Comté, there are two examples: one is tarte aux asperges – a baked egg custard containing slices of white or green asparagus; the other is eggs which are scrambled with diced asparagus stalks, and the tips are used as decoration. In America, incidentally, President Thomas Jefferson was an asparagus admirer, growing it at his home in Virginia in the late 1700s.

Hollandaise sauce, meanwhile, is an emulsion of egg yolk and clarified butter, whisked in a bain-marie over a gentle heat, and with a hint of acidity to its taste. It is rich, creamy and buttery, and that acidity comes from the use of lemon juice. The sauce is possibly a French creation, and in *Le Cuisinier François* (1651), François Pierre La Varenne provides a recipe that calls for butter, vinegar, salt, nutmeg and egg yolk to bind it. It sounds distinctly hollandaise by ingredients if not by name. Of France's recipe books in the mid-18th century, *Les Dons de Comus* offers two versions of the sauce, one made with egg yolk (as we know it today), the other does not include the yolk, and is made with butter, a little flour, bouillon and herbs. Both are for sauce 'Hollondaise'.

There are disputes, however, over the provenance of hollandaise. Was it, for instance, originally Sauce Isigny, named after the town in Normandy where the good quality of butter is renowned? Or should we believe another suggestion, that the French Huguenots brought it from the Netherlands when they returned to their homeland? Béarnaise sauce is certainly French, and derives from hollandaise, but calls for tarragon (and sometimes chervil), shallots and white wine vinegar instead of lemon juice. Delicious with beef.

Whatever the case, eggs Benedict is not eggs Benedict without hollandaise. And it is the perfect sauce to spoon over asparagus – which has been steamed or dropped into salted boiling water for a few minutes – and a poached egg or two. Many accomplished chefs who are able to create the most complex of dishes, still choose this simply-crafted combination as one of their favourites.

PIZZA

Tomato, mozzarella and herbs on a dough base, baked in the fierce heat of a wood-fired oven. Other toppings optional. Swooned over by Italians, and crooned over by Dean Martin: 'When the moon hits your eye like a big pizza pie, that's amore ...'

Who better to talk pizza than Francesco Mazzei, chef-proprietor of Sartoria in London's Savile Row? 'Can you imagine a world without pizza?' he says, shuddering slightly at the thought. 'It would be like a world without espresso. Pizza is light, affordable, and can be eaten wherever and whenever – over a romantic meal or when you're watching the football on TV.'

Only a few, inexpensive ingredients are required. In fact, it costs about as much to make a dreadful pizza as it does to make a great one. The dough should be light and, says Mazzei, give some thought to the tomato sauce:

'Don't use fresh tomatoes. Instead, pass tinned tomatoes through a sieve, or mouli, into a bowl. Add to this, one clove of crushed, chopped garlic – no more than that – a torn fresh basil leaf, dried oregano, extra virgin olive oil and a little salt. Cover the bowl with cling film, let the mixture marinate overnight. Tomorrow morning, spread this mixture onto toast. Eat it, and call me ...'

The cheese should be a high-quality mozzarella. Next there is the temperature of the wood-fired oven. 'I like it to be about 380°C,' he says.

'A pizza should take no more than a minute to cook. It should be slightly burnt around the edges, and the underside of the base should have ashes on it, with the mozzarella bubbling. All of this adds flavour. Do you know what – a pizza is something which spreads happiness. It will make you feel happy just to smell it and see it. If it doesn't have that happy feel about it, then eating it won't make you happy. When it is right, when the dough is light, it is also a gourmet dish.'

Mazzei does not see the need for embellishments such as pineapple, sweet corn or chicken (pizza bianca has no topping). 'So many people have tried to change it, but why? It is a food that will never die. It will continue for as long as there is a future, and as long as there is Italy there is pizza.'

The ancient inhabitants of Mediterranean countries, not only Italy, ate flat bread with toppings, and the word possibly stems from pitta, the Arab bread. The pizza, however, is said to come from Naples. Then it is a napoletana. And the most basic version of the napoletana is topped with tomato sauce, oregano and garlic. It is also known as marinara because sailors (*marinai*) would take it on voyages, sailing from the city's port, happy at least that they had a stash of pizzas which would keep for a while.

*

The royal seal of approval works wonders for dishes, and such was the case, apparently, in June 1889 when Margherita, the queen of Italy, paid a visit to Naples.

Here, the tale is taken up by *The Washington Post* of the time:

Queen Margaret is in Naples at the palace of Capedimonte, and a story is related of her which explains the secret of her popularity among the people. A favorite eatable with the Neapolitans is the pizza, a sort of cake ... that is in a round form, and seasoned with various condiments. The Queen sent for a pizzaiolo

who is famous for his skill in making these cakes, as she said 'she wanted to eat like the poor people'.

The man went to the palace, was received, and having shown a list of thirty-five varieties of pizza, was sent to the royal kitchen to make the kind which the Queen had selected. He made eight which were the ideals of their kind, and the little Prince and his mother found them excellent, but to eat as the poor people in Naples eat – that is often not at all, and is more than could be expected. But she has visited the poor quarter of Naples, and sympathizes with the misery she sees there.

It is acknowledged that the pizza-maker (or *pizzaiolo*) was Raffaele Esposito, and his winning creation was named Margherita; tomato sauce with mozzarella, basil and oregano, as described by chef Mazzei. Esposito's winner was an edible salute to the red (tomato), white (mozzarella) and green (basil) of the *Il Tricolore*, the Italian flag.

In 2012 it was disputed that Esposito had actually been the pizzaiolo who made the Queen's pizza. Zachary Nowak, the assistant director of Food Studies at the Umbra Institute in Perugia, investigated the story. He concluded that Esposito had indeed received permission to put the royal seal above his shop during the royal visit, but at the time it was a wine shop and not a pizzeria.

Nowak also questioned the letter of thanks from the Queen's secretary Signore Galli to Esposito. 'The letter bears the royal seal. Or does it?' asked Nowak.

A careful comparison of the seal shows that it is very similar but not identical to the various royal seals of the period. Even more obvious to even the casual glance is that the seal is quite off-centre and several degrees off the vertical axis. Unlike all the other royal correspondence of the day – which had seals printed on them, not rubber-stamped on like the Galli letter – this seal appears at the bottom centre, not on the top left. The words 'House of her Royal Majesty' is handwritten on the top of the letter, leaving us to believe that the queen had run out of stationery.

The phenomenal success of the pizza in America began with the influx of Italian immigrants in the early 1900s, many of them settling along the Eastern seaboard. The country's first pizzeria was opened by Gennaro Lombardi in New York's Spring Street in 1905. Others soon followed, and the pizza would evolve.

The *Encyclopaedia of American Food and Drink* points out:

The ingredients these immigrants found in their new country differed from those in the old. In New York there was no buffalo-milk mozzarella, so cow's milk mozzarella was used; oregano, a staple southern Italian herb, was replaced in America by sweet marjoram; and American tomatoes, flour, even water, were different. Here pizza evolved into a large, sheet-like pie, perhaps eighteen inches or more in diameter, reflecting the abundance of the new country.

The beginning of Britain's affection for pizza roughly coincides with the opening of the first Pizza Express, in Soho's Wardour Street, in 1965. Today the chain has about 400 restaurants around the globe, and the business is valued at about £1 billion. A world without pizza is unlikely.

FOR AFTERS

ICE CREAM SUNDAE

Balls of ice cream, drizzled with syrup, adorned with a cherry and nuts. Born in America, but where and how?

Three places in the United States of America feature in the peculiar story of the ice cream sundae, taking us from Wisconsin to Illinois and New York. More than a strong whiff of rivalry surrounds the claims of ownership over this dessert.

Let us begin in Two Rivers, on Lake Michigan, in Wisconsin. In 1881, it is said, one George Hallauer wandered into Berner's Soda Fountain. He asked the owner, Edward Berners, to drizzle chocolate syrup over the ice cream. 'Are you crazy?' said Berners, or words to that effect. 'That syrup is for the sodas.'

However, he agreed to Hallauer's request. At that moment the sundae was born. This led to a booming trade in the novel dish, which Berners cheerfully sold at a nickel a time. He started selling them on Sundays before realising he was onto a winner and so made them and sold them every day.

There are counter claims which question this account, notably the argument that Ed Berners was a teenager in 1881 – too young, therefore, to have his own business.

This takes us to Evanston, in Illinois, and the early 1890s. A law was introduced which prohibited the sale of sodas on a Sunday. Ice cream therefore was served instead, with soda syrups poured over it and – hey presto! – the 'Sunday' was born. However, Methodist ministers objected to the dish taking its name from the Sabbath. Hence the ice cream Sunday became the ice cream sundae.

Meanwhile, the residents of Ithaca, New York, have gone to enormous trouble and effort to prove that their town is birthplace to the sundae.

Ithaca's tourism website states that its information and documentation is so specific that the city can almost pinpoint the exact hour the first ice cream 'Sunday' was served: 'While other cities may claim the sundae, none can support its claim with primary evidence.' Ithaca's evidence now follows.

On the afternoon of Sunday, 3 April 1892, Reverend John M. Scott finished his service at the Unitarian Church and then wandered downtown to the Platt & Colt Pharmacy. The pastor was a regular at the shop, and the proprietor, Chester C. Platt, was the church treasurer.

The two men often met for a chat on Sundays. On this particular one, as they sat chatting, Platt turned to his fountain clerk, DeForest Christiance, and said: 'DeForest, please bring us two bowls of ice cream.' When the ice cream – vanilla, it is said – was placed in front of them, proprietor Platt topped each with cherry syrup and a candied cherry.

In 1936, DeForest wrote a letter to the city's resident historian John Brooks, in which he addressed the event. He recalled that when the two men:

… Tried out this new concoction they became very enthusiastic about its flavor and appearance, and immediately started casting about for a suitable name. It was then that Mr Scott said, why not call it Cherry Sunday in commemoration of the day on which it was founded. This name appealed to Mr Platt, so from that day on we served Cherry Sunday, and later on Strawberry, Pineapple, Chocolate etc.

Photo: i.rene.m.hsu

His letter continued: 'The new Sunday became very popular with the student trade, so when they went home for their vacations they naturally told their local druggists about it, which soon spread the name throughout the country.'

DeForest concludes that shortly afterwards, 'One of the fruit syrup manufacturers came out with the name Sundae, and later a competitor with it spelled Sunda or Sundi. The original, which I am satisfied was first prepared and named in the old Platt & Colt was, as you know spelled Sunday.'

There is also documentation to show that in 1894 Platt & Colt tried to patent the Sunday. The request was turned down on the grounds that the shop had no intention of shipping the Sunday abroad and it was therefore not entitled to such protection. Add to this, a newspaper advertisement in the *Ithaca Daily Journal* of 5 April 1892, a couple of days after the creation: 'Cherry Sunday. A new 10 cent ice cream specialty served only at Platt & Colt's famous day and night soda fountain.' This is the first-known mention in print of the ice cream. And on Monday, 11 April, beneath the news that a hunter had shot a wild goose in the marsh, there is this paragraph:

'Platt & Colt's soda fountain specialty is Cherry Sunday. It is ice cream served in a champagne glass with cherry juice syrup and candied French cherries on top.' By 1894, and the failed attempt at trademarking the 'Sunday', the fruit syrup manufacturer, it seems, had swapped a 'y' for an 'e' to avoid potential legal action; and was selling syrups to be drizzled over the ice cream.

The knickerbocker glory – an ice cream sundae in a tall glass – is also the cause of confusion. There are many theories for how it got its name. To me, the most probable is that is was named after the Knickerbocker Hotel, in Manhattan, which opened in 1906 and closed in 1920, as a result of Prohibition. It was grand and opulent, tall (sixteen storeys), and with a pink and cream facade. The Knickerbocker was also home to an extremely popular café where, I imagine, the ice creams included the glorious Knickerbocker.

A brief mention of Britain. From the early 1850s, 'iced cream' or 'street ices' were sold by street vendors (who included entrepreneurial dairy farmers). In the parks and markets of London, there were the cries: 'Raspberry cream! Iced raspberry cream, ha'penny a glass!' You would be given the ice cream in a small glass, and ate it with your fingers or slurped it. Many of them were trying ice cream for the first time, and remarked upon the feeling that 'it had snowed in their bellies'. Then you would hand back the glass, which was 'cleaned' in dirty, cold water and was ready to be filled for the next customer. Disease spread through this unhygienic method of feeding.

In 1851, one commentator wrote that street ices 'were somewhat of a failure last year ... but this year they seem likely to succeed'. A hundred years later there were 20,000 ice cream vans in Britain – a number that would decline once supermarkets mastered the ice cream trade.

TRIFLE

A British dessert comprising layers of custard (sometimes sherry-soaked); sponge; jam or jelly; and whipped cream. Often decorated with chopped nuts, such as almonds or walnuts, and presented in a large glass bowl.

Trifle was a dessert waiting to happen. Before its arrival, the British had syllabub and fool, the ancestors of the trifle.

Syllabub is a mixture of cream and alcohol – sweet wine, sweet sherry or sweet cider – and was a drink taken as a dessert before it thickened and needed a spoon. The fool is a mixture of cream and fruit, often gooseberries or damsons.

Today, we whisk the cream for both dishes. Whisking takes just a minute or two, thanks to the power of electricity. In earlier times, whisking was an exhausting, time-consuming chore and probably something of a culinary skill. Thus, the cream for both syllabub and fool was rarely whisked. Cookery books talked of 'stirring' to achieve a thick consistency. Far easier to heat the cream by the fire, and often the fool was made like this; cream baked with sugar. Much fruit was also thought to be poisonous, so the fool would have to wait for it to be included.

The origin of syllabub's name is unknown, but the dish is easy enough to make. Whisk 300 millilitres double cream with 75 grams caster sugar, but be careful not to over-whisk it. Add the juice of a lemon and 60 millilitres sweet wine or sweet sherry. Spoon into six tall-ish glasses. Place in the fridge to chill. Once chilled, serve.

We start to see the use of the word 'trifle' (from the Old French trufle, meaning small) during the reign of Elizabeth I. In *The Good Huswife's Jewell* (1596), Thomas Dawson gives this recipe for trifle: 'Take a pint of thicke cream and season it with suger and ginger, and rosewater; so stir it as you then would have it and make it lukewarm on a dish on a chaffinge dish and coales, and after put it into a silver piece or a bowle, and so serve it to the borde.' Although he called it a trifle, it was more like a fool and so it had some way to go. (By the way, the 'borde' or board was a table, as in a piece of wooden board. When playing cards, if you kept your hands above the table, rather than underneath it, you were certainly not a cheat – instead, you were 'above board', decent and honest.)

Trifle, as we know it, came in the 1700s, and in the publication – pivotal in British gastronomy – of *The Art of Cookery, Made Plain and Easy*, by 'A Lady'.

That lady was Hannah Glasse who was born in Holborn, London, in 1708, married an Irish soldier and together they worked as domestic staff in at least one aristocratic household. Hannah had financial problems and, in her late 30s, was sent to debtor's prison. Clearly, she was a woman of great resolve, writing the recipes which she felt deserved a wide audience. A decade later, in 1747, she saw the publication of *The Art of Cookery*. It was a best-seller, with twenty editions published before the turn of the 19th century. All of this, while bringing eleven children into the world.

Her brilliant book partly illustrates the British love of cream at that time. She gives, among others, recipes for lemon-cream, orange-cream, barley-cream, almond-cream, and even steeple-cream, which begins with the instruction: 'Take five ounces of hart thorn and two ounces of ivory, and put them in a stone bottle, fill it up with fair water to the neck …' For 'everlasting syllabubs' – made with German wine and sack, as well as thick cream, the juice of Seville oranges and lemon rind – she asks the reader to, 'beat it well together with a whisk half an hour'.

But she has a cooking tip: 'The best way to whip syllabub is have a large, fine chocolate mill, which you must keep on purpose, and a large, deep bowl to mill [the syllabubs].' The chocolate mill was what we might call a cocoa grinder which, as it revolved, thickened the syllabub.

Hannah Glasse's recipe for trifle is short and almost as sweet as the dessert:

Cover the bottom of your dish or bowl with Naples biscuits broke in pieces, mackeroons broke in halves, and ratafia

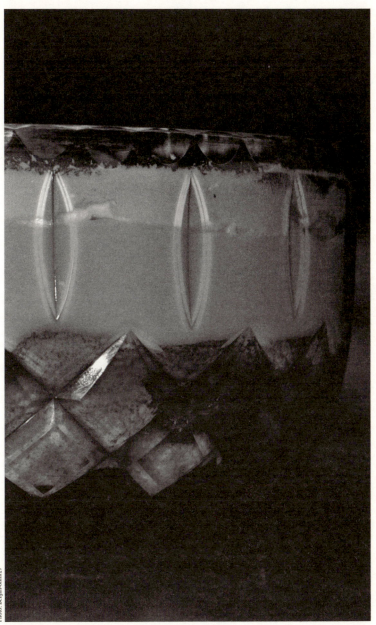

cakes. Just wet them all through with sack and then make a good boiled custard, not too thick, and when cold pour it over, and then put syllabub over that. You may garnish it with ratafia cakes, currant-jelly and flowers.

Glasse's currant-jelly is, in fact, more like jam. The trifle, subsequently, was made with jelly. Did cooks think they were sticking to Glasse's recipe by using 'jelly'?

In 1861, Isabella Beeton uses jam in her recipe (in *Household Management*) but introduces the notion of jelly: she suggests jam in the trifle, but that the whipped cream topping should be adorned with bright currant jelly (or crystallised sweetmeats or flowers). There may also have been American-British jam-jelly confusion which led to the substitution: American cooks used jelly when they were supposed to use jam.

Whatever the reason for the switch from jam to jelly, it is jam which makes the superior trifle. Use a couple of jars of black currant jam, heated in a saucepan with a little sherry, before allowing it to cool and then use as a layer of the trifle. Chantilly cream is the finest topping: whip 500 grams double cream with 50 grams caster sugar and the seeds of one vanilla pod. Flaked almonds, toasted for a moment under a hot grill, are an ideal ornament.

BLACK FOREST GÂTEAU

Layers of kirsch-soaked dark chocolate sponge; sour, pitted cherries; a lavish covering of Chantilly cream and chocolate swirls. Baroque in style, but 20th-century German in origin.

There is the cake and then there is the gâteau. The cake is the manly one: think of a sweaty, sword-wielding Viking, reaching British shores, clambering over the side of his boat and yelling, 'Kaka! Kaka!' He was screaming for what we now call cake. Norsemen gave us that much-used word.

Cake is confusing. At times it is close in taste and cooking technique to bread and bun. Meanwhile, oatcakes are cakes but are also surely biscuits because they are flat and brittle. And the puffed up Eccles cakes (from the little town on the outskirts of Manchester) were not always sweet: once they were made with a filling of calf's foot, as well as currants and spices.

Gâteau, by comparison, is elegant and beautiful. She has layers – light and never too thick – of sponge, and offers pure indulgence. That palatable pleasure may be in the form of sweet creams, iced fondants, fruit jellies or semi-sweet chocolate ganache. Or perhaps it is the appealing taste and scent of a liqueur.

While the cake fills a hole the gâteau brings a smile. The Victorians could not get enough of gâteaux. The larger the gâteaux and the taller they towered, the more impressive they were. Nothing has changed. Pâtissiers in Paris were lured across the English Channel in the 19th century to feed the fashion of London's socialites. (Today many apprentice pâtissiers in Paris go to Tokyo to learn the art of pastry.)

The French-ness of Black Forest gâteau is to be found only in its name because this is a delight from Germany. There, you should ask for a slice of Schwarzwälder Kirschtorte (Black Forest Cherry Tart).

Some say this gâteau was born in Berlin, shortly before the Second World War. More convincing is the claim that it was created in 1915 by Josef Keller, a pastry chef in Café Ahrend in Bad Godesburg, on the west bank of the Rhine and not

Photo: Fahimaru

far from Bonn. After the First World War he opened his own café in his home town of Radolfzell, on the banks of Lake Constance. He trained August Schaefer during the 1920s and later gave his recipe book to his protégé. It contained the original recipe for the gâteau. Sour cherries and kirsch are products of the Black Forest and were readily available to Keller. He lived and worked close to the region of evergreen forests and ever-ticking cuckoo clocks.

Black Forest gâteau became a hit on the American dinner party circuit of the 1960s, and in the States is known as Black Forest cake. Its success in the United Kingdom has been phenomenal, achieving great notoriety as a dessert when, throughout the 1970s, it seemed to feature on every single British restaurant menu. It was up against the cheesecake, tinned fruit cocktail and gala melon 'boat' (which was served as both a starter and dessert).

*

In my travels over the years I have asked accomplished, well-known chefs and cooks about their favourite cakes. Cornwall-based Nathan Outlaw opts for Battenberg ('because I'm a lover of marzipan, which also accounts for the extra four or five stone I carry around') while Pierre Gagnaire chooses tarte Tatin. Nobu, meanwhile, told me: 'My father died when I was a kid and his brother brought some strawberry shortcake at Christmas time. I eat almost any cake but that's my favourite.'

Torta de Santiago de Compostella, the almond tart from Galicia, wins the vote from Giorgio Locatelli and the esteemed food writer Claudia Roden.

Jason Atherton has a recently-acquired obsession with carrot cake: 'I'll sit down with a cup of tea and a slice of carrot cake and marvel at the way a cake can be made with carrots. It fascinates me.'

The masterful Anthony Demetre is equally smitten and fascinated. 'Even before I first ate carrot cake, I loved it. Just the thought of carrots in a cake intrigued me.' He is coeliac, but says: 'I've now managed to make a spanking one that's gluten free.'

Victoria sponge is another favourite, as is Black Forest gâteau because, as Claude Bosi says: 'You have sweet, acidity and bitterness and the alcohol. Everything in one cake.'

APPLE PIE

A British classic dating back to medieval times: lightly spiced, sweetened apples within a pastry case.

The apple arrived in Britain, it is believed, during the Neolithic period (4,000–2,500 BC) but was not a popular feature in the diet. It took the Roman invasion in the 1st century AD to muster up an interest in the fruit. The Romans introduced sweet cultivars. They were also knowledgeable about pollination and the wisdom of orchards.

When the Romans left Britain, the interest in apples faded and it was only after the Norman invasion that more orchards were created, particularly in the grounds of monasteries and wealthy landowners. The Normans gave us 'sidre', the Old French for cider. By the 14th century, it was used and cooked frequently in recipes. *The Forme of Cury*, compiled by Richard II's chief chefs, contains recipes for fritters of parsnips and apples, as well as 'tartis in applis', apple tart. 'Take good apples, and spices and figs,' it advises, cover them in saffron and bake in 'a cofyn', which was the pastry case and not, in those days, supposed to be eaten.

Inevitably, the apple became a staple. Hardy and easy to grow, it was even easier to steal in large quantities and sell. The costard was a variety which was often sold by street vendors and, in time, costard mongers became costermongers, sellers of fruit and vegetables. Rummaging around beneath the apple trees in orchards, you might find the shrivelled apples, known as 'scrump' (stemming from Swedish), and if you thieved them then you were 'scrumping' (the word did not make it into the dictionaries until the 19th century).

The apple pie benefitted from a few factors in economic and social evolution: sugar became cheaper; spices became more available; and the pie crust became edible – the dish was more enjoyable to eat. Soon it would make its way to America where, eventually, it would become as American as the hot dog and burger. Across Europe, the apple with pastry is eaten: France has its tarte Tatin, Austria has its apple strudel, apple streusel cake is eaten in German homes, and Danish pastries are popular across the continent.

Few odes to food are as passionate as 'Apple Pye', penned by Dr William King (1663–1712). He was an English judge, author and poet, as well as a great gourmet. He hoped to publish a *Biblioteca Culinaria, or The Cook's Complete Library*, but died before it could be achieved. However, during his lifetime he wrote prolifically of food. He noted that cooks '… are not of the most patient disposition', though he was a man who loved to cook and who pondered culinary intricacies and strived to share the knowledge he acquired.

'A good dinner,' he also believed, 'is brother to a good poem; only it is something more substantial, and between two and three o'clock, more agreeable.'

Of all the delicates which Britons try
To please the palate or delight the eye,
Of all the sev'ral kinds of sumptuous fare,
There is none that can with apple pie compare.

When first this infant dish in fashion came,
The ingredients were but coarse, and rude the frame.
And yet unpolished in the modern arts,
Our fathers ate brown bread, instead of tarts.
Pies were but indigested lumps of dough,
Till time and just expense improved them so.

King gives a tremendous salute to 'godlike' Edward of the Saxon line, whom he credits (heaven knows why) as refining the pie – quinces were added, the pies crusts were trimmed and cream was introduced as an accompaniment. Yet King provides insight into the 17th-century apple pie.

Draw out your dough elaborately thin,
And cease not to fatigue your rolling pin.
Of eggs and butter, see you mix enough,
For then the paste will swell into a puff …
Ranged in thick order let your quinces lie,
They give a charming relish to the pie.
If you are a wife, you'll not brown sugar slight,
The browner (if I form my judgement right)
A deep vermillion tincture will dispense,
And make your Pippin redder than the quince.
When this is done there will be wanting still.
The just reserve of cloves and candy'ed peel.
Nor can I blame you if a drop you take,
Of orange water, for perfuming sake.
But here the art of nicety is such

There must be not too little, nor too much …

Half a century later, Hannah Glasse would have agreed with King's words. Her recipe calls for a squeeze of lemon, a blade of mace, and suggests 'you may put in a little quince or marmalade, if you please'.

It is best to avoid 'cooking apples' as they require lots of sugar to sweeten them. Cox's Orange Pippin and Granny Smith are ideal varieties for apple pie.

DOBOS TORTA

A chocolate gâteau topped with caramel, and served in the cafés of Budapest.

This extravagant gâteau takes its name from its creator József C. Dobos (1847–1924), a skilled pastry chef and confectioner in 19th-century Budapest. Dobos was a colourful character, connoisseur and gourmet. Perhaps the Escoffier of Hungary.

Dobosh, as the cake is also known, consists of five thin, round layers of sponge, with fillings in between of coffee-laced chocolate buttercream. The shiny, dark, glistening top is a glaze made of caramel.

Dobos, it is said, acquired the buttercream recipe during a trip to France. His cake received its debut at the Hungarian National Exhibition, which took place in 1885, and achieved further notoriety when it became fashionable after receiving the royal seal of approval.

However, the creator refused to share his recipe. Inevitably, this led to copies which were not always so similar to the

Photo: Edsel Little

original. Clearly proud of his conception, Dobos travelled around Europe, baking the cake and showing it off at special parties. He also managed to write a few cookery books.

In later life, he donated his recipe to the Budapest Bakery Guild and Confectioner's Chamber of Industry, enabling the original to be shared with fellow members of his profession.

In New Orleans, the multi-layered doberge cake was inspired by the dobosh, and created in the 1920s by the baker, Beulah Ledner. In *New Orleans Memories: One Writer's City*, Carolyn Kolb writes: 'The first change Mrs Ledner made was in the name – "dobos" doesn't sound very French, and knowing that Orleanians loved their French pastries, she cleverly settled on "doberge" – which sounds about the same.' The doberge cakes are usually chocolate or lemon flavoured, and covered in buttercream, followed by a coating of icing.

CRÈME BRÛLÉE

… In French. To the British, it can also be burnt cream or Trinity cream. Vanilla-infused custard is baked and crowned with a brittle caramel glaze.

This dessert is petite but has plenty of drama, and to be eaten, it needs to be broken into.

Just as an egg is cracked, this sweet, egg-rich pudding – usually cooked and served in a ramekin – has a topping of dark, crunchy caramel, which needs to be broken with the tap or three of a dessert spoon. Voilà! Theatre at the table. Beneath the fragments of sweet glaze there is a pot of silky indulgence:

a smooth, vanilla-speckled mixture of double cream, egg yolks and sugar, which has thickened during baking.

It is so good that it has almost threatened the Entente Cordiale between France and Great Britain: each country claims to have invented it.

In the early 18th century, recipes for 'burnt cream' began to appear in British cookbooks. It also featured in *The Experienced English Housekeeper* (1769), Elizabeth Raffald's hefty, compelling book of some 800 recipes – or 'receipts', as they were known – many of them appealing to the sweet-toothed reader. (Raffald was born and raised in Doncaster, and wrote that she had 'spent fifteen years in great and worthy families in the capacity as a housekeeper, and had an opportunity of travelling with them, but finding the common servant so ignorant in dressing meat, and a good cook so hard to be met with, put me upon studying the art of cookery …')

Her recipe for burnt cream is certainly crème brûlée, even if it does have the addition of lemon peel, egg whites and orange flower water. It goes like this:

Boil a pint of cream with sugar, and a little lemon peel shred fine. Then beat the yolks of six and the whites of four eggs separately. When your cream is cooled, put in your eggs, with a spoonful of orange flower water and one of fine flour. Set it over the fire. Keep stirring it 'till it is thick. Put it into a dish. When it is cold, sift a quarter of a pound of sugar all over, hold a hot salamander over it 'till it is very brown and looks like a glass plate put over your cream.

We also know this dish as Trinity cream, after Trinity College, Cambridge, where it has been served for many

centuries. There, a branding iron is used to imprint the college crest on the cream, which is served in a large bowl and not ramekins. Sometimes it is known as Cambridge burnt cream. At Cambridge, when the crest is not used, the brûlée top is cracked and whole raspberries are tossed onto the cream, a delicious and colourful twist which adds flavour, acidity and texture.

However, in France the term crème brûlée was used in print in 1691 by François Massiolot, chef to (among others) Philippe I, Duke of Orléans and brother of Louis XIV, and his son, Philippe II, who was a bit of a show-off at the stove and liked to cook for his mistress, a countess, and her staff.

François Massiolot later gave a recipe for crème anglaise (or crème a l'anglaise). This 'English cream', or custard, is similar to the one used for brûlée – suggesting perhaps that crème brûlée is indeed burnt (English) cream. (Crème anglaise also forms the yellow 'sea' in îles flottantes – the classic French dessert of poached meringues in custard, again served cold. This crème is a versatile base which can be flavoured with rum or liqueurs such as kirsch or maraschino, as well as chocolate, or infusions of coffee or tea.)

In the 1800s the British began to call this dessert crème brûlée, preferring its elegant, poetic mystique and the charm of all things French. In recent years British restaurant menus often revert to burnt cream. Whatever the name, the dish is easy to make but simple to get wrong.

*

Digressing for a moment on the subject of coffee, Louis XV was a renowned philanthropist. During a lengthy reign (1715–1774) his seduction technique involved rustling up pots of astonishingly good coffee. Even more impressive, the coffee was not only made by him, but also grown by him, in the botanical gardens at his Palace of Versailles. He roasted it, too. The wondrous whiff of the monarch's roasted beans enticed scores of soon-to-be mistresses to visit his chambers.

And to think that only a century or so earlier, coffee was the subject of complaints from priests to Pope Clement VIII – they condemned it as the 'bitter creation of Satan'. Pope Clement, a true Florentine, shooed them away. He happened to love his coffee, so much so that he blessed it. This horrified the priests but ensured that from that moment Catholics could happily drink it and sleep well at night. Or not, depending on their level of caffeine consumption before bedtime.

*

Making crème brûlées is a good way for the cook to train her- or himself to think in terms of proportions and ratios of ingredients.

Mastering this technique can remove the necessity to have a cookery book at your side in the kitchen. Recipes and quantities of ingredients will become easy to remember.

Begin by breaking down the recipe of crème brûlée as if cooking for one. So the ingredients for one crème brûlée are:

1 egg yolk
1 dessert spoon caster sugar
½ cup double cream
Plus, vanilla and sugar for the glaze.

Is that easier to remember than a recipe for six? After that, it is merely a matter of multiplication to get to the amount of ingredients needed, depending on the number of guests.

To make crème brûlée for six …

Preheat the oven to 140°C.

Pour three cups of cream into a saucepan. Add two vanilla pods, split lengthways and halved. Gently bring them to the boil.

Remove the pods. On a plate or plastic chopping board, use a teaspoon to scrape out the vanilla seeds. Return the seed and the pods to the hot cream, allowing them to infuse for fifteen minutes.

In a large bowl, mix six eggs with six dessert spoons of caster sugar.

Remove the pods from the cream and bring the cream back to the boil. When the cream bubbles, pour it into the bowl, whisking constantly (to avoid scrambled egg).

Return this egg-cream mixture to the saucepan. On the lowest heat, stir until the custard is thick enough to coat the back of a wooden spoon (rather than running off it).

Remove the pan from the heat. Pour the custard through a fine-meshed sieve into a jug. Pour the custard from the jug into six ramekins, filling each one by three quarters.

Create a bain-marie in which to bake the brûlées. To do this, line a large, deep roasting tin or Pyrex dish with cardboard (a brown cardboard box is ideal). Place the ramekins on top of the board. Pour recently boiled water into the tin/dish so that it comes halfway up the side of the ramekins. Carefully – so as not to let the water spill into the ramekins – place the roasting tin in the preheated oven. Bake for about 40 minutes.

Allow the brûlées to cool before placing them in the fridge to chill.

At least an hour before serving, place the ramekins on a baking tray. Sprinkle caster or brown sugar over the brûlées.

Place the baking tray under a hot grill so that the sugar browns and caramelises. Or use a cook's blow torch to achieve the same effect, browning from the outside and working towards the centre.

Allow the caramel to cool. Sprinkle over another layer of sugar. Repeat the caramel process, under a grill or with a blow torch.

Allow to cool before serving, though never in the fridge as the glaze will melt.

The custard can be made well in advance, of course, and stored in the fridge, covered with a layer of cling film on the surface to prevent a skin forming.

Note: The bain-marie prevents the brûlées overheating and obtaining a 'grainy' thickness. But they can be made without use of a bain-marie, by being baked for 50 minutes in an oven preheated to the lower temperature of 100°C. The cream can be replaced by a mixture of half milk, half cream.

CHEESECAKE

Conceived in Greece in ancient times, this is a much-loved dessert in Britain and an American icon. Smooth creamy top on a crunchy base.

Cheesecake was a favourite of the ancient Greeks. It is believed that athletes ate it before competing in the first Olympic Games (776 BC), and this type of cake was popular at weddings and celebratory feasts. Fresh feta cheese was pounded until smooth, and then mixed with honey.

The Romans added eggs and flour to the recipe, and possibly bay leaves. They called it *libum*, and introduced the cake to other parts of Europe. In England, *The Forme of Cury* (the 14th-century recipe book compiled by Richard II's chefs) has this recipe for 'tart de bry': semi-soft cheese is mixed with egg yolks, ginger, sugar, saffron and salt; the mixture is spooned into a pastry shell and then baked.

Elizabeth Raffald observed in the 1700s: 'A moderate oven bakes them best. If it is too hot it burns them and takes off the beauty, and a very slow oven makes them sad and look black. Make your cheesecakes up just when the oven is of a proper heat and they will rise well and be of a proper colour.'

What we now know as cream cheese was created in the 1870s, and became an essential ingredient in the New York-style cheesecake, now an iconic American dessert. It is said that a New York dairyman called William Lawrence accidentally made the first cream cheese as they were trying to replicate French Neufchatel. Inadvertently, Lawrence produced a cheese which was rich and creamy enough for him to name it cream cheese. The Empire Cheese Company

of New York began producing the Philadelphia brand of cream cheese.

This brand was acquired by James Kraft, who devised a method of pasteurising cheese, keeping it well preserved and enabling it to be exported. Born in Ontario, Kraft began his cheese business in Chicago with $65 and a rented horse-drawn wagon. Today the Kraft Heinz company has sales of $27 billion.

The best cheesecakes are made from a simple recipe, very much like this one …

Serves 6

Ingredients

110 grams crème fraîche
800 grams cream cheese
110 grams caster sugar
1 egg
1 vanilla pod, scraped
120 grams digestive biscuits
50 grams butter, melted

Pre-heat the oven to 150°C.

In a large bowl, mix the crème fraîche, cream cheese, sugar, egg and vanilla seeds.

Crush the biscuits. Heat the butter in a saucepan or on a low setting in the microwave. Mix the biscuits and butter.

Place the crushed, buttery biscuits in the bottom of a twelve-centimetre baking tin, and spread evenly. Spoon the cheese mixture on top of the biscuit base and spread it evenly.

Bake for 25 minutes in the oven. The cheesecake should not colour during cooking.

Note: Vanilla bean paste is excellent and widely available in supermarkets. Use one dessertspoon of the paste instead of the seeds of one vanilla pod. The paste is sugary; so if using reduce the amount of sugar in this recipe to 100 grams.

BAKLAVA AND TURKISH COFFEE

A sweet taste of the Ottoman Empire; thin pastry, nuts and syrup.

The Turkish have an old proverb: 'The heart seeks neither coffee nor the coffee house; the heart seeks a friend. Coffee is just an excuse.'

The Turkish are devout coffee drinkers, and their coffee is strong. It is served with a glass of water, there to cleanse the palate before drinking the coffee.

They were ahead of the British with their coffee culture. The first coffee houses of the Ottoman Empire were opened in the 1530s, in Aleppo and Damascus, and then in the Turkish capital, Istanbul, in 1554 (about a century before England's first coffee house).

Traditionally, a piece of Turkish delight (*locum*) was eaten, to remove the bitterness of the coffee. Another Turkish saying

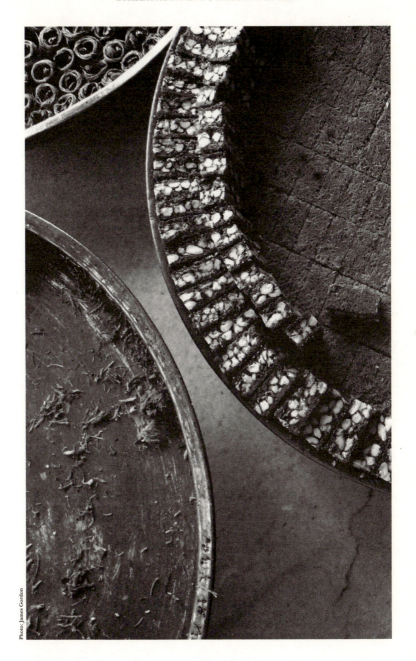

goes: 'A cup of bitter coffee brings 40 years of friendship.' That was at a time when coffee was made without sugar. As sugar became more readily available in the 1700s, it became an ingredient in the coffee-making process. So the coffee is sweet, but Turkish delight is still served in keeping with the custom.

Turkish coffee is made like this: two cups of drinking water are poured into a *cezve* (Turkish coffee boiler); add two teaspoons of fine ground coffee and sugar to taste; over a low heat, stir the coffee and when froth appears it is poured into cups; the remaining coffee is boiled and poured when it froths.

To tell the fortune of a coffee drinker: when the coffee is finished, hold the cup above the drinker's head and rotate it. The cup, not the head. Then turn the cup upside down on a saucer as the drinker simultaneously makes a wish.

You need to look at the traces of ground coffee in the cup and on the saucer to assess the future for the coffee drinker. Seeing mountains means travel, a fish suggests the drinker will become wealthy, a bird symbolises the imminence of news, and a horse means the drinker's wish will come true.

All of this can take place while taking bites of a slice of baklava, the sweet and nutty pastry of the Middle East.

Nuts – pistachios, walnuts, almonds – are pounded with cardamom and the zest of lemon and/or orange until coarse (not powdery), and coated in melted butter. The nutty mixture is spread between thin sheets of filo pastry and baked at about 160°C. Then the pastry is brushed with syrup – made with sugar, water, a little rosewater and lemon juice. This is followed by a second baking at 190°C, for just a few minutes to fasten the syrup glaze. Honey can be used instead of syrup, or blended with the syrup.

Baklava's origins may lie in either of these dishes: the Ancient Greek *plakous* (cheese and honey between layers of pastry) or the Turkish dessert *güllaç* (layers of nuts and honey between filo pastry) which features in the 14th-century book of food, drink and medicine by Hu Sihui, physician to the Mongol court.

PAVLOVA

Whipped cream and fruit in a large shell of meringue. Beautiful and celebratory. But should it be berries or kiwi fruit, and was it really created in the Antipodes?

Ligovo is an ancient suburb in the south of St Petersburg and is where, in February, 1881, a young, unmarried laundress called Lyubov gave birth to a daughter, Anna. The father's identity remains a mystery, although there have been suggestions that he was a Jewish banker. Lyubov married one Matvey Pavlov, providing Anna with a stepfather, and with the surname she would adopt; a name that would also come to be associated with one of the world's great desserts, Pavlova.

By the age of eleven, Anna Pavlova was appearing in ballet on stage. Slightly awkward in pose (a small body with long legs) she was nicknamed 'The Broom' by fellow students, but she was chosen for the Imperial Ballet. From there, young Anna became a sensation. She was swooned over by critics and audiences.

She is best known, perhaps, for her creation of the Dying Swan in the penultimate movement of *The Carnival of the Animals*. Over the course of her career she performed this dance some 4,000 times … and, of course, with her notoriously weak ankles. (On her deathbed she whispered: 'Bring my swan costume.')

In 1912, Anna moved to Britain, and to North London, settling in a large house – complete with a small lake and swans, of course – in Golders Green. By now she was a successful touring prima ballerina, travelling around the world to perform on stages with her own dance company.

And that is what she did in 1926, when she boarded a ship and began the five-week voyage to Australia, heading first to Melbourne, where fans had travelled hundreds of miles to see her. She was a hit. From there, she went to Sydney, greeted at the railway station by thousands of onlookers. And after a few weeks of performing in Sydney she sailed with her ballet company to New Zealand. There, she performed in a theatre in Wellington and stayed – pertinent to this story – in a hotel in the city.

At some point, before she returned to Australia to complete the tour, the hotel's chef presented her with 'The Pavlova Cake'. Or so the story goes. In Australia, meanwhile, it is claimed the dish was created during the ballerina's second Australian tour in 1929.

For decades the two countries have squabbled over the pavlova, each adamant that the dessert was created on its shores.

*

Among those squabbling were Dr Paul Wood, a New Zealander academic, author, art historian and culture critic, and Annabelle Utrecht, an Australian with a background in media and also owner of a food retail outlet.

Their disagreement arose in 2014, during a conversation on Facebook, when Annabelle claimed the pavlova cake to be an Australian dessert. Andrew pinged a response, declaring it was New Zealand's culinary achievement, referring to the publication of a pavlova cake recipe in the *New Zealand Dairy Exporter* annual on 10 October 1929. Their cyberspace row was driven by national pride and they set out to prove each other wrong.

A few days later they touched base, this time in a more conciliatory fashion. They had both stumbled upon evidence which seemed to point to an entirely different point of origin from what they had always taken for granted: that pavlova was an antipodean 'invention'.

They became a pair of pavlova fanatics, and teamed up to research the origins of the dessert. On their database of recipes, they have amassed 2,300 pavlova-related entries. And they are writing a book about their adventure and their discoveries. The working title is *Beat It Stiff: The Secret History Of The Pavlova.*

Annabelle, the Miss Marple of meringue, recalls:

From the outset it was clear that the pavlova cake was neither an original dessert presentation, nor a southern hemisphere innovation. To be honest, we were both shocked by that initial revelation and it set us on a course of dedicated research. Two and a half years have passed now, and we've uncovered an entirely new history to the pavlova dessert.

Until the project began, she did not often eat pavlova.

My mother is German and emigrated to Australia in the late 1950s. Mum is a wonderful cook, who wastes nothing and believes you must respect ingredients and always cook with love. I once watched her walk away

Photo: jules: stone soup

hungry from a sandwich shop and asked why she didn't purchase one. Her answer was straightforward, 'They didn't make them with love.'

In terms of desserts, mum's repertoire was more likely to include traditional Germanic sweets like strudel, streusel kuchen, yeast cakes or vanillekipferl (although she has become somewhat legendary in the lamington department over the years). Growing up, my favourite desserts were those of my mother's, or aunts – often simple things like apple pancakes, Berliner, cherry clafoutis or flaugnardes. But if a slice of pavlova came my way, I'd happily consume it!

Annabelle made her first pavlova in her twenties (for an Australia Day celebration) but did not bake another until the great pavlova research project began. 'Technically though,' she says, 'I don't make pavlovas. I only bake the recipes we would call a pavlova today – those which have been hidden in historic cook books under alternate names. I should make a significant point here. The pavlova is merely a rebranding of an historic cake that has been in existence for a very long time.'

*

And so she took me through the pavlova files:

'Our research has revealed that the cake we call a pavlova today, was in existence for at least a century before any Antipodean recipes emerge.

'In fact, large-form meringues topped with whipped cream and fruit were not only present in the European and North American culinary dialogues, but quite fashionable during the 19th century. And they became even more popular at the turn of the 20th century. Of course, they were not called "pavlova" then. Rather, they manifested under a variety of equally charming or practical epithets.'

Petite meringues filled with whipped cream and fruits can be found in European recipe books dating back to the 18th century, says Annabelle:

'The larger scale meringue constructions filled with combinations of whipped cream, nuts or fruit preserves – sometimes referred to as "ornamental cakes" – begin to commonly reveal themselves in the early 19th century recipe books of the Austro-Hungarian empire and other German-speaking lands. We say German-speaking lands because Germany as a nation did not exist until 1871.'

The Spanische windtorte (a very fancy meringue cake filled with flavoured whipped cream and fruit) emerged from the royal court of the Habsburgs, and not long after, pavlova-like cakes begin to appear in Europe under various names.

These include tourte aux meringues, baisertorte and a variant of the schaum Torte (German for foam cake.) These incredibly time-consuming and elaborate manifestations, she says, were originally the product of aristocratic kitchens. Quickly, they became popular dishes with the well-heeled, making their way into the cookbooks of the Germanic middle-classes.

Throughout the 18th and 19th centuries, political and economic turmoil in Europe motivated waves of mass migration into the United States. Between 1820 and the First World War, almost 6 million Germans migrated to the USA

– and with them came their crafts, traditions and, of course, recipe books.

Annabelle continues: 'By the 1860s, what emerges in areas of dense Germanic settlement, like the US Midwest, is the presence of cakes identical in every way to the pavlova of today. In fact, the modern American schaum torte is still a beloved and extremely popular regional dessert in US states like Wisconsin and Iowa.'

By the first decades of the 20th century, meringue concoctions like the schaum torte, began to appear on menus around America, but with Americanised names such as kiss cake, fruit meringue and cream meringue.

Meanwhile, says Annabelle, the British were making elegant, large-scale meringue cakes. Just like the pavlova, these were topped with whipped cream and fresh fruit. One of the dishes was Portman Meringue, named after a viscount in the aristocratic Portman family.

The recipe was published in 1909, *The Cookery Book of Lady Clark of Tillypronie*, some twenty years before Anna Pavlova visited the Antipodes. Indeed, the recipe stems from a period between 1841 and 1897. (There were similar recipes at the time, says Annabelle, including one called Strawberries Meringue.)

'It's identical to a pavlova in every way. It tells us that this type of meringue dessert was now *trending* in the northern hemisphere. It was more than a cake, it was vogue – a sign of domestic superiority, social sophistication and haute-table fashion.'

*

Their research has led them back even further, to the Austro-Hungarian Habsburg dynasty and the politics of that period. 'The Habsburgs,' says Annabelle, 'had a fascination for all things Spanish. It was a romantic association with the origins of their family-lineage. And what emerges in cookbooks of that period, are hundreds of "Spanische" titled recipes. The Spanische windtorte is just one of these themed dishes.' The windtorte is a cylinder of meringue filled with cream and fruit and topped with a meringue 'lid'. It can be garnished with flowers.

'In German, windtorte means "wind-cake", a reference to driving wind into meringue batter – in other words, aerating the mixture. It is not, as some have suggested, a reference to windflower, a species of anemone. Windflower is toxic and should never be used in cookery.'

From the 1780s, Spanische-wind related recipes appear in cookery books, all of them sophisticated meringue dainties of some description. By the 1790s a glut of Spanische windtorte recipes were published in Germanic cookery books.

*

In the 1880s, housewives in Australia and New Zealand were able to buy a product called Duryea Maizena, an early name for cornflour or cornstarch. Says Annabelle: 'Food industrialists like William Duryea quickly recognised the value of publishing corporate recipe booklets which promoted their brand directly to cooks and housewives alike.

'When it comes to a corporate cookery book which included references to meringue tarts and meringue tourte, the first and earliest example Dr Wood and I came across was *Recipes for the Use of Duryeta's Maizena: An Article of Food that Received Two Prize Medals At The International Exhibition, London, 1862*. It was published in New York in 1864.'

The significance of Duryea's recipe book is twofold. First, it reveals the names of several fashionable 1860s meringue dainties including Maizena floating islands (baked meringues on custard), Maizena meringues, Maizena meringue tarts, Meringues à la crème, and under the heading 'Gateaux et Patisserie au Maizena' (Cakes And Pastries from Maizena) are Meringues au chocolat and Tourte meringues (known to be a large-scale meringue torte topped with whipped cream and fruits).

Second, it shows that the addition of cornflour to meringue recipes is not an independent antipodean innovation, as has been suggested by some. Rather, it was one of several well-known meringue formulas published and promoted by northern hemisphere food industrialists during the 19th century.

With this in mind, the claims are clearly wrong that Australian or New Zealand home cooks advanced meringue mixtures by incorporating cornflour. It is more likely that commercial recipes such as Duryea's Maizena were available in the southern hemisphere, and that cornflour-inclusive meringue recipes reached Australian and New Zealand via commercial booklets and product packaging recipes.

Annabelle says: 'The first-known "Pavlova Cake" recipe, published in New Zealand in October 1929, contained a ration of cornflour. This gives us a vital clue as to its true origins – which we will disclose in our book. The second published recipe for a pavlova cake in 1933 also contains a cornflour component, but by 1934 pavlova cake recipes often contained none.'

She adds:

'I would like to make one slightly snarky point, if I may, with regard to the Wellington legend. Dr Wood and I have discovered many pavlova-named desserts and dishes dating between 1911 and 1930. Without exception, we can identify each of their chef-authors or venues of creation. They are the product of haute cuisine or commercial agreements, and their presence in the culinary dialogue corresponds with the movements of Anna Pavlova.

'If there had indeed been a Wellington "invention" in 1926, why was there was no reporting or documentation of the dish? Why can we not find a Kiwi chef-candidate to claim it? And why did it take until 1929 for the first recipe to emerge? The answer, we believe, is that this dessert was not a Kiwi innovation.'

She continues: 'You might be interested to know that a legend exists in Australia, that the pavlova was invented in Melbourne in 1926 by a chef at the Menzies Hotel – and unlike Wellington's claim, there is some anecdotal evidence which supports the production of at least one Anna Pavlova-homage dish on menus at the Menzies.'

She and Dr Wood can confirm that New Zealand has the first recorded 'Pavlova Cake' recipe in a publication (1929) – 'but this does not mean that it is a Kiwi creation. To us, this recipe appears to have just landed in New Zealand and without proof of a creator or a venue of creation, the recipe is unlikely to have birthed from New Zealand's loins in 1929 – because in that year, Anna Pavlova only toured Australia.

'I must stress again though, that the pavlova is merely a rebranding of a very popular northern hemisphere dainty, and given we have now discovered dozens of never-before documented, pavlova-named desserts and dishes, there is the very real possibility, that the pavlova belongs to neither New Zealand or Australia. Indeed, it looks to us, as though this cake was born elsewhere.'

Significantly, their evidence suggests that large meringue cakes topped with whipped cream and fresh fruit existed in Australia and New Zealand much earlier than that first 1929 'Pavlova Cake' recipe, and that the rise in popularity of the pavlova-style presentations in the southern hemisphere, follows the culinary trends already in progress in the northern hemisphere.

Typically, northern hemisphere recipes arrived in Australia and New Zealand via cookery books, newspapers, promotional ephemera and through culinary skill and cultural exchanges between cooks or housewives. Ocean liners and the age of syndicated media also allowed recipes to travel quickly from one side of the globe to the other, and we know that the pavlova proto-type was present in Australia, well before it had that name.

*

Does she ever get sick of pavlova?

'I never get sick of researching the pavlova, pavlova-named dishes, pavlova-like dishes, the chefs who created them or the venues of their creation. Large scale meringue cakes in particular, are not just dishes, rather, artifacts with geopolitical, technological and societal associations. Likewise, Anna Pavlova-food homages are windows into celebrity, culture, food-ways, industry, haute cuisine and the ending of Edwardian-era plenty, as the privations of Great War loomed. It is a mistake to look at a dish's evolution, separate to history – and for that reason the genre of pavlovas deserve full chronicling.

'Since beginning this project, I have become absolutely enchanted by olde-worlde cookery and I must confess, I also love attempting these recipes. Whether it's an 18th century Spanische Wind dainty, or the Davis Gelatine "Pavlova" recipe (a colourful, four layer jelly published first in Australia in 1926) – I can't resist the challenge and when you go to the trouble of recreating these gorgeous old recipes, you learn a lot.

'Once I hand-beat egg whites and sugar for 45 minutes with two forks bound together, because I wanted to know how labour intensive and time consuming meringue-making must have been before the advent of rotary beaters. Turns out – aerating meringue that way is hard. My froth thickened, but never fully stiffened. It was still usable though, and when spread on wafers and baked, I understood how special a dish like that would have been in the 16th century.'

Annabelle always samples the historic cakes that she bakes, and tends to give away the rest of the cake for others to 'review'. She says: 'One of my favourite things, is hearing, "That pavlova was amazing."

'It's my cue to cheekily jump in and reply, "Thank you, but it wasn't a pavlova … because pavlovas weren't around in the 1840s."'

ACKNOWLEDGEMENTS

Dear reader, I am extremely grateful to you for taking the time to dip into *The 50 Greatest Dishes of the World*. You could have picked another book to read at this very moment. Yet you chose this one. Thank you, sincerely.

Many have contributed to the creation of this little feast. Fine chefs and cooks, gifted authors and journalists, ever-hungry gourmets and gourmands: each has added a touch of this or a splash of that.

At Icon Books, Duncan Heath has been encouraging and supportive. He remained confident that one day – eventually – the manuscript would arrive. He was right, as you can see. My editor Ellen Conlon has been brilliant and wise, and it has been an honour to work with her.

Thanks to Gavin Morris, the designer, Sara Bryant, who was tasked with reading the proofs and correcting errors, and Victoria Reed, who handled the publicity.

Charlie Brotherstone, as excellent a literary agent as he is a lunch companion, is sick of me thanking him. But I shall do so nevertheless.

Ken Hom has guided me through the food of China and South-east Asia (kindly providing a gorgeous recipe for Peking Duck). Francesco Mazzei, chef-patron of Sartoria in London's Savile Row, has been my Italian inspiration. Those grand chefs from France, Raymond Blanc and Michel Roux, have helped me to appreciate fully the joys of their national cuisine.

Three decades after we first met, Marco Pierre White remains a close friend and mentor, always willing to assist as I write about food. While I worked on this book, he invited me to stay at his cosy hotel, Rudloe Arms in Wiltshire, and fed me incredibly well.

Adam Byatt is chef-patron of Trinity, in Clapham, South-west London. For those who live north of the Thames, Trinity is *the* reason to cross the river. Adam has been a rich source of know-how and culinary cleverness.

I am also indebted to Isabelle Augier for her help with caviar. And thank you so much, Armen Petrossian, for your valuable insight into the delicacy.

Regarding beef Wellington, Lucinda Ebersole sent old recipes. Meanwhile, Stephen Henry, the esteemed executive chef at the Palmer House Hilton in Chicago, scoured the hotel's archives. Thank you for whooshing me back to the golden age of gastronomy.

Annabelle Utrecht was also generous with her time, explaining to me the extraordinary story of pavlova. Annabelle, I can't wait to read your book. To Mississippi master-cook Melissa Magnuson, I plead Oliver Twist-style – *please, please may I have some more gumbo?*

I must also thank Diane Sequeira for curry advice, and for her chicken curry recipe. Caroline and Emily Maddick put me up at their beautiful villa in Mallorca, where I could make gazpacho and paella, drink and eat them … and write about them for this book. Roger Pizey, the renowned pastry chef, has frequently helped answer my questions about desserts and puddings. Cheers Rog. Oh, and Craig, Sarah and Georgina Cooper – thank you, and what great timing!

Thank you to the four special people who have been there throughout, putting up with me and my cooking: Louise, Charlie, Billy and Daisy. Let's go for lunch.